# MR. LINCOLN

# THE NEGROES

# MR. LINCOLN

# &

# THE NEGROES

## *THE LONG ROAD*
## *TO EQUALITY*

⸻

# WILLIAM O. DOUGLAS

Orville

*ATHENEUM* NEW YORK
1963

# FOREWORD

IN APRIL, 1961, I shared a platform in Washington, D.C., with Tom Mboya of Kenya, the theme of the rally being "Free Africa." I spoke briefly, reading part of the Declaration of Independence and giving Lincoln's commentary on it. A few days later a senior officer of the State Department, who had represented the United States in Asia and the Middle East, commented to me on the news account of the rally.

"You have misread the Declaration of Independence," he said.

"In what way?"

"The Declaration of Independence," he replied, "only announced that Americans were equal to British subjects. It had nothing to do with racial problems."

I listened with amazement. "I had supposed, Mr. Secretary, that Lincoln won that argument a century ago."

Since the ideas of white supremacy seem to linger on even in high places, I concluded that all of us should know more about the Great Debates of the 1850's and 1860's.

*v*

I have made Lincoln's Second Inaugural, delivered March 4, 1865, my chief point of reference, as it contains an eloquent summary of the main political events leading to the Civil War. Moreover, that address—which came shortly before one door was closed on war and another was opened on the struggle for civil rights—established the philosophical basis for the political contest which was to follow. In this country various ideas of "equality," as among people of different races, had been much mooted during the debates of the 1850's and 1860's. The idea of "equality" contained in the Declaration of Independence was projected throughout public discussions while the Civil War progressed. The Gettysburg Address, November 19, 1863, indeed proclaimed that this nation was "dedicated to the proposition that all men are created equal." The Emancipation Proclamation, January 1, 1863, had given that idea wings. But in the setting of 1863 that Proclamation was quite a different document from what it later became in 1865.

The Emancipation Proclamation, like the Magna Charta, has become a symbol of freedom and equality which was no part of it in the beginning. Lincoln conceived of it as a military measure. It indeed freed only some slaves, not all of them. Soon, however, it was the rallying point for complete emancipation both in this country and abroad where slaves and serfs worked for masters of the same or different race. It became particularly symbolic of the struggle of the Negro in this country for political rights—the right

to vote, to hold office. The theme of the emancipation has continued to grow until it now includes social equality.

Abroad under colonial regimes the ideas of political and social emancipation have reached demanding
and at times violent proportions. The modest demands of Lincoln have expanded in the popular
mind to include matters to which he had seldom addressed himself. In the Great Debates of 1858, Lincoln himself denied the existence of any claim on his
part to social equality of the Negro:

"I protest, now and forever, against that counter-
feit logic which presumes that because I did not want
a negro woman for a slave, I do necessarily want her
for a wife. My understanding is that I need not have
her for either, but, as God made us separate, we can
leave one another alone, and do one another much
good thereby. There are white men enough to marry
all the white women, and enough black men to marry
all the black women, and in God's name let them be
so married."

He envisaged the Negro's political rights as the
product of gradualness. In the debates of 1854 he
stated: "Let it not be said that I am contending for
political and social equality between whites and
blacks. I have already said the contrary."

In 1857 he referred to the Declaration of Independence as a maxim "for free society, which should
be familiar to all, and revered by all; constantly
looked to, constantly labored for, and even though

never perfectly attained, constantly approximated, and thereby constantly spreading and deepening in influence and augmenting the happiness and value of life to all people of all colors everywhere."

Lincoln, a good lawyer as well as a good politician, never posed issues unnecessary for the immediate decision. But by the time he won the 1860 election the *New York Times* concluded that he proposed for Negroes "a perfect equality of civil and personal rights under the Constitution"—as the Constitution then read.

Of course at that time the American public, North as well as South, was far from accepting the Negro as a co-citizen. In only a few states (Maine being one) were Negroes allowed to vote. The 1862 constitution of Illinois provided that no Negro or mulatto could migrate to or settle in that state, nor have the right to vote nor to hold any office. Before those restrictions were lifted in 1865, a number of Negroes were convicted in Illinois courts for living there; and were *sold to the highest bidders* to pay fines assessed against them!

Thus the environment in which Lincoln lived and practiced law, though not tolerating the institution of slavery, relegated the Negro to second-class citizenship. John C. Calhoun of South Carolina looked on that *status quo* as a permanent one:

"The difficulty is in the diversity of the races. So strongly drawn is the line between the two in consequence, and so strengthened by the force of habit and education, that it is impossible for them to exist together in the same community, where their numbers are so nearly equal as in the slave-holding States, under any other relation than that which now exists. Social and political equality between them is impossible. No power on earth can overcome the difficulty. The causes lie too deep in the principles of our nature to be surmounted. But, without such equality, to change the present condition of the African race, were it possible, would be but to change the form of slavery. It would make them the slaves of the community instead of the slaves of individuals, with less responsibility and interest in their welfare on the part of the community than is felt by their present masters. . . ."

As recently as 1955 one judicial opinion expressed the view that segregation of the races was the proper way of life:

"I might venture to point out in this connection that segregation is not a new philosophy generated by the states that practice it. It is and has always been the unvarying law of the animal kingdom. The dove and the quail, the turkey and the turkey buzzard, the chicken and the guinea, it matters not where they are found, are segregated; place the horse, the cow, the sheep, the goat and the pig in the same pasture and they instinctively segregate; the fish in the sea segregate into schools of their kind; when the goose and duck arise from the Canadian marshes and take off for the Gulf of Mexico and other points in the south, they are always found segregated; and when God created man, he allotted each race to his own continent according to color, Europe to the white man, Asia to the yellow man, Africa to the black man, and America to the red man, but we are now advised that God's plan was in error and must be reversed despite the fact that gregariousness has been the law of the various species of the animal kingdom."

This view—which is opposed to the Supreme Court's 1954 decision on the segregation of the races in public schools—was an ancient one even in Lincoln's day. His greatness lay not merely in the rejection of that view. He was a politician and statesman —a man who, while adhering to principle, moderated his pace or hurried it as public opinion kept up with him. His role was to inform the public, educate them, lead them. His task was to marshal the men and women of good will everywhere behind the maintenance of one United States of America. In the beginning his strategy was to preserve the Union and to move either slowly or fast to that goal, depending on what was practical. Later his strategy was to rid the nation of slavery. In his early years he was not ready to grant Negroes political equality. In his later years he was consumed in an effort to show our people that the basic need of a multiracial community is equality for all.

While the frame of reference of the struggle for "equality" is different from what it was in Lincoln's day, the opposed views have not greatly changed. The idea of emancipation has acquired, however, new and different meanings as the years have passed. Today around the world emancipation has become synonymous with social and political equality. And though politicians declare that all men are equal and though it is an article of faith in America, England, France, India, Israel, and a few other nations, the idea persists in most nations that somehow or other some men are more equal than others.

I have collected in the Appendix the main documents that highlight the controversy from the beginning of this nation to the 1960's.

I am indebted to Paul E. Ogle, Sr., of Allentown, Pennsylvania, for letters throwing new light on the Republican Convention of 1864. And I owe special thanks to Joan C. Martin and Dagmar Hamilton, whose researches made my path easy.

WILLIAM O. DOUGLAS

# MR. LINCOLN

# THE NEGROES

# ONE

W HEN THE SUN ROSE MARCH 4, 1865, ON
Washington, D.C., rain was falling. By nine
o'clock it was pouring down. During the downpour
mounted troops sat on their sleek horses in front of
the White House, ready for escort duty. They wore
white gloves; their boots were polished; their suits
were freshly pressed. By ten o'clock crowds lined
the streets leading to the Capitol. Though the rain
continued, the people did not seem to mind. This
was Inauguration Day in the midst of a war. In spite
of the rain, in spite of a cold raw wind, they came
out to see and hear a man they loved.

While Washington, D.C., had sidewalks, the streets
leading to the Capitol were not paved. As a result
of the storm, the mud was nearly ten inches deep.
People's shoes were covered with it; and they tracked
it onto the sidewalks, which were soon covered with
a thick, slippery paste. The rain drove through men's
coats and soaked women's dresses. The ladies' skirts
were muddy; their velvet and lace grimy, but they
too stayed to see the parade.

The horses which brought the Presidential carriage from the White House to the Capitol galloped all the way.

Police headed the parade, walking through the mud. Next came the marshal and his aides on horseback. A battalion of Negro troops dressed in Union Army blue marched through the rain and the mud as an honor guard.

The Marine Corps, other troops of the Union Army, and many bands were present.

The old soldiers of the American Revolution and those who fought in the War of 1812 took part. Lincoln Clubs participated, as well as clubs supporting the new Vice-President—Andrew Johnson. Representatives of states and cities and various fraternal and benevolent associations marched. One float carried the model of a navy boat on which a cannon was mounted. It was attended by sailor boys, who fired the cannon over and again cheering lustily each time. The Washington, D.C., Fire Department paraded its vehicles, followed by firemen from Philadelphia. A labor union arranged for typesetters to operate a hand press on a float. As the parade moved along, men turned the printing press and threw pamphlets to the spectators—pamphlets containing the program of the day's events, the order of procession, an article concerning the Inauguration, and an Inaugural poem dedicated to the President and Vice-President.

In spite of the cold and the mud, the rain-soaked public were in a holiday mood and gave the parade a rousing reception. Among those cheering from the sidelines were former members of the Confederate Army who had left the South to join the North.

The first part of the Inaugural ceremonies took place in the Senate Chamber. Many people, most of them women, jammed the galleries; among them was the President's wife. Down below sat the Cabinet, the Supreme Court, members of the Diplomatic Corps, and Members of the House and Senate. Senator Solomon Foot of Vermont presided. The President sat in the front row.

The first item of business was administering the oath of office to the new Vice-President. As the clock struck twelve, Andrew Johnson was escorted into the chamber and introduced by the outgoing Vice-President, Hannibal Hamlin. Johnson then delivered an address and took the oath of office, his hand upon the Bible. That ceremony over, everyone moved outdoors again for the rest of the program.

The plaza of the Capitol was by now packed with rain-soaked people. Some had stood for hours awaiting the event. A sea of uplifted faces greeted the man returning to the White House for another four years as their President.

The Inaugural Address, his second one, was printed in two columns on a single sheet of paper. As he held it in his hand and started reading, the sun burst through the clouds for the first time that day. In the open sky a bright star, probably Venus, was shining.

He stood six feet four inches—the height he had reached when he was seventeen years old. Some who attended the 1860 Convention that nominated him for President had called him "a long-legged, unknown lawyer from Illinois." His hair was dark, unruly, crumpled. His face was wide-boned and plain, filled with wonder touched by sorrow. Though over fifty years old, he was lean, strong, and fit. Yet his strength—gained largely with the ax in early years—seemed dedicated to gentle tasks. It was strength to preserve, not to destroy—power applied with firmness in the cause of humanity.

His voice was well modulated for public speaking. But there were no loud-speakers in 1865 and, of course, no radio. A gusty wind prevented his voice from carrying to the edges of the crowd.

"Fellow countrymen: At this second appearing to take the oath of the presidential office, there is less occasion for an extended address than there was at the first. Then a statement, somewhat in detail, of a course to be pursued, seemed fitting and proper. Now, at the expiration of four years, during which public declarations have been constantly called forth on every point and phase of the great contest which still absorbs the attention and engrosses the energies of the nation, little that is new could be presented. The progress of our arms, upon which all else chiefly depends, is as well known to the

public as to myself; and it is, I trust, reasonably
satisfactory and encouraging to all. With high
hope for the future, no prediction in regard to it
is ventured."

# TWO

H E HAD MARRIED MARY TODD OF LOUISVILLE, Kentucky, in 1842 when he was thirty-three years old. She was a daughter of a wealthy Louisville family. Her friends tried to dissuade her, saying, "He is mighty rough, slack-skinned, lank, clumsy, with a craggy head of coarse black hair. . . . Any fool can see he is a small town lawyer, nothing more. His kin are poor white trash."

But she was headstrong and had her way.

They had four sons, Robert, Edward, William, and Thomas (Tad). Edward died when young; so it was a family of five at the time the people elected a President in 1860.

The President-elect, his wife, Mary Todd, and their sons, Bob, Willie, and Tad, left Springfield, Illinois, on February 11, 1861, for Washington, D.C. They traveled by train scheduled to leave at 8 A.M. It was a wet, misty morning and about a thousand people came out to see them off. The locomotive was a small one with a flat-topped smokestack. It had but two cars—one for baggage and one for the Presidential party. He had not planned to make a speech. But, as he stood on the rear platform to say farewell to his friends, he took off his hat, raised his hand for silence, and said:

"My friends—No one, not in my situation, can appreciate my feeling of sadness at this parting. To this place, and the kindness of these people, I owe every thing. Here I have lived a quarter of a century, and have passed from a young to an old man. Here my children have been born, and one is buried. I now leave, not knowing when, or whether ever, I may return, with a task before me greater than that which rested upon Washington. Without the assistance of that Divine Being, who ever attended him, I cannot succeed. With that assistance I cannot fail. Trusting in Him, who can go with me, and remain with you and be every where for good, let us confidently hope that all will yet be well. To His care commending you, as I hope in your prayers you will commend me, I bid you an affectionate farewell."

The locomotive bell rang and the train moved east, his friends standing at the station, their faces wet with tears. Everyone knew that troubled days lay ahead. Oncoming events that no one could predict were to cause even more sorrow than had been expected. Before a year had passed, Willie died and the father, standing over the body of the boy, choked with emotion and could only say, "We loved him so."

On December 20, 1860, South Carolina had seceded. Before the President-elect even reached the Capitol to take the oath of office, the United States was fast dissolving.

Many in the South wanted to form a new nation, calling it the Confederacy and making slavery its cornerstone. There were plans even to restore the African slave trade that had been outlawed.

Robert B. Rhett of South Carolina was one of those who wanted to establish a new government founded on slavery. "If we are not fighting for slavery, then what are we fighting for?" he asked. Largely as a result of his efforts, delegates assembled on December 20, 1860, at a convention in Charleston, South Carolina, and voted for secession from the Union.

Because fifteen states had slavery, the Charleston convention adopted a flag with fifteen stars. The new Confederate government, in Rhett's words, was to be "a great slave-holding Confederacy, stretching its armies over a territory larger than any power in Europe possesses." Jefferson Davis was elected President of the Confederacy, a constitution was adopted, and Montgomery, Alabama, was chosen as the new Confederate capital.

There was some sentiment in the North to let the South go its own way. Horace Greeley, abolitionist and editor of the New York *Tribune,* had written on November 9, 1860, "If the cotton states shall decide that they can do better out of the Union than in it, we insist on telling them go in peace. . . . We hope never to live in a republic whereof one section is pinned to the residue by bayonets."

In December, 1860, and in January and March, 1861, there were proposals in Congress for a settlement of the slavery issue by compromise.

One idea was to amend the Constitution so as to deprive Congress of the power to abolish slavery.

Another proposal was to amend the Constitution barring slavery north of latitude 36° 30′—roughly north of a line stretching from Norfolk, Virginia, to Wichita, Kansas—but allowing it below that line both in territory then in the United States or later included in them. Objections were raised that this proposal would include Cuba and Mexico, which might then be incorporated in the United States as slave territories.

Others proposed that territories of the United States be given the power to determine by their territorial legislatures whether they would or would not have slavery.

While the President-elect would have paid slaveowners to free their slaves, he was against these compromises.

On December 10, 1860, he wrote a letter to a Senator saying:

"Let there be no compromise on the question of *extending* slavery. If there be, all our labor is lost, and, ere long, must be done again. The dangerous ground—that into which some of our friends have a hankering to run—is Pop. Sov. [Popular Sovereignty]. Have none of it. Stand firm. The tug has to come & better now than any time hereafter."

He tried to allay fears that his administration would directly or indirectly interfere with slavery. On December 22, 1860—just two days after South Carolina had seceded—he wrote: "The South would be in no more danger in this respect than it was in the days of Washington." He went on to say that he realized that those assurances were not enough. "You think slavery is *right* and ought to be extended; while we think it *wrong* and ought to be restricted. That I suppose is the rub. It certainly is the only substantial difference between us."

Conditions between North and South worsened. By the time the President-elect reached Washington, D.C., seven states had seceded—Alabama, Georgia, Florida, Louisiana, Mississippi, South Carolina, and Texas. He said, "I only wish I could have got to Washington to lock the door before the horse was stolen. But when I get to the spot I can find only the tracks."

By June, 1861—three months after he became President—eleven states had seceded, and the capital of the Confederacy was moved to Richmond, Virginia. Yet, before that happened, the power of the federal government was greatly weakened. The federal mint for coining of money located in New Orleans and two smaller mints were seized by the Confederacy. Of the 1,108 officers in the regular army of the United States, 387 resigned to join the Confederate Army. Robert E. Lee, one of the greatest, had decided to stand by the Union if Virginia did, but to follow her if she seceded. When Virginia seceded (April 17, 1861), he resigned to take charge of the Army of Virginia. In his letter of resignation Lee stated, "Save in the defense of my native State, I never again desire to draw my sword. . . ."

Of the seventeen or more forts maintained by the federal government in the South, all but Fort Sumter, which was located on a rocky island three miles out from Charleston, South Carolina, were seized at once by the Confederates. The federal government also had many arsenals in the South and dozens of custom houses, post offices, and lighthouses. When the seceding states seized all of these the President was presented with a difficult problem. Should he try to retake all that federal property?

The issue quickly shaped up at Fort Sumter, which was garrisoned by federal troops under the command of Major Robert Anderson. Charleston, which supplied Fort Sumter with food, was now cut off. The existing supply would last only until April 15. South Carolina sent word to the President that if he attempted "to reinforce Sumter," war would break out; the only way to prevent war was for him to acquiesce in secession.

He would not approve of secession, as that would be the end of the Union which he was pledged to preserve. He had promised in his First Inaugural that "The power confided to me will be used to hold, occupy, and possess the property and places belonging to the Government. . . ." Yet he was anxious to prevent the nation from plunging into war.

He decided to try to provision Fort Sumter without use of force. Only if that attempt were resisted would force be used. Word of this plan was sent to Jefferson Davis, whose advisers were divided as to what the Confederacy should do. Davis decided that Fort Sumter should be attacked by Confederate forces. On April 11, a note was sent to Anderson at Fort Sumter asking for its surrender. Anderson refused. The Confederates, knowing Anderson would soon be out of food, sent four men to Fort Sumter near midnight on April 11, again asking for its surrender and requesting that Anderson set a date for its evacuation. Anderson consulted with his officers until 3 A.M. April 12 and finally told the four emissaries he would evacuate the fort at noon on April 15. The emissaries replied that the Confederates would "open fire" on Fort Sumter in one hour.

An hour later batteries of artillery let loose on Fort Sumter. Though the ships filled with provisions were close to Fort Sumter, they could not approach the fort. The artillery fire continued for thirty-three hours. On the night of April 13 Anderson agreed to surrender. On April 14, he marched his garrison out and the Confederate flag—at that time representing Alabama, Florida, Georgia, Louisiana, Mississippi, South Carolina, and Texas—was hoisted over Fort Sumter. The next day, April 15, 1861, the President by proclamation called out the militia of the states, directing that they report to Washington, D.C., and retake the forts and other property seized from the federal government.

Virginia seceded April 17, Arkansas May 6, Tennessee May 7, and North Carolina May 20.

On April 18, Virginia's troops seized Harpers Ferry, which was then a federal fort and arsenal. On April 20 the federal navy yard at Norfolk, Virginia, was threatened and the officer in charge, to prevent seizure by the Confederates, burned it. Confederate troops were now west of the nation's capital at Harpers Ferry and south of it at Norfolk. The rail lines north ran through Baltimore, Maryland. Though that state was not secessionist, it had many southern sympathizers, who seized the telegraph office in Baltimore, tore up railroad tracks, and blew up railroad bridges. It appeared that Washington, D.C., was being threatened.

On April 18, 532 militiamen from Pennsylvania arrived in Washington. On April 19, a Massachusetts regiment, after skirmishes in Baltimore, reached the capital. On April 25, a crack New York regiment arrived. Then came troops from Rhode Island and more from Massachusetts. Ten thousand Union troops now guarded the city.

People in Richmond, Virginia, only 122 miles south of the capital shouted, "On to Washington!" People in Washington, D.C., shouted, "On to Richmond!" Many Northerners felt that if Richmond could be quickly taken the war might end quickly. Public pressure for attacking the Confederates increased. The North soon had 225,000 troops; and of these 30,000 were in the Army of the Potomac pushing south into Virginia. Some generals of the Union Army thought more time was needed to train the raw troops under their command. The President overruled the generals, saying, "You are green it is true, but they [the Confederates] are green also." On July 21, 1861, a Union army moved into battle against 21,900 Confederates at Bull Run and the Civil War was under way.

"On the occasion corresponding to this four years ago, all thoughts were anxiously directed to an impending civil war. All dreaded it—all sought to avert it. While the inaugural address was being delivered from this place, devoted altogether to *saving* the Union without war, insurgent agents were in the city seeking to *destroy* it without war—seeking to dissolve the Union, and divide effects, by negotiation. Both parties deprecated war; but one of them would *make* war rather than let the nation survive; and the other would *accept* war rather than let it perish. And the war came."

# THREE

T HE WAR HAD NOT COME IN AN ATTEMPT TO FREE the slaves. The immediate cause of the conflict was the spread of slavery, a topic which had been the central issue of the 1860 campaign.

Forty years earlier—in 1820—Congress passed a law which provided that Missouri might come into the Union with slavery, but that no other territory north of latitude 36° 30' should ever have slavery. Under that arrangement no future slave states would have been admitted to the Union except those occupying the territory which now makes up Oklahoma, New Mexico, Arizona, and the southern part of California.

Years passed, the settlement of the West continued, and California and New Mexico became populated. In 1849, California asked for admission as a state but was refused, primarily because her constitution excluded slavery. The South wanted certain concessions if California was to come in as a free state. As a result a new compromise between the slave-holding states and the free states was worked out.

Both sides benefited from this Compromise of

1850. For the sake of the South, a new law was passed, with more effective provisions for the return of fugitive slaves who escaped to the North. For the sake of the North, slave trade in the District of Columbia was abolished. To please the South, legislation was enacted provided that Utah and New Mexico could enter the Union with or without slavery, whichever they chose. To please the North, Congress provided that California might come in as a free state.

Lincoln argued in many speeches during the 1850's against these compromises and against the extension of slavery into new territories. " 'If I have a field,' " he quoted, " 'around which the cattle or the hogs linger and crave to pass the fence, and I go and tear down the fence, will it be supposed that I do not by that act encourage them to enter? *Even the hogs would know better*—Much more *men,* who are a higher order of the animal world.' "

In 1854, Congress had passed a law to form a territory out of what is now Nebraska and Kansas. That law contained a proviso that the people who went there to settle could establish slavery or exclude it, as they saw fit. He opposed that law: "But if it is a sacred right for the people of Nebraska to take and hold slaves there, it is equally their sacred right to buy them where they can buy them cheapest; and that undoubtedly [*sic*] will be on the coast of Africa. . . ."

British courts took a different view of slavery from American courts. In 1772 Lord Mansfield discharged a Negro held in London as a slave by a Virginian who intended to bring him back to this country. Lord Mansfield said:

". . . The state of slavery is of such a nature, that it is incapable of being introduced on any reasons, moral or political; but only positive law, which preserves its force long after the reasons, occasion, and time itself from whence it was created, is erased from memory: it's so odious, that nothing can be suffered to support it, but positive law. Whatever inconveniences, therefore, may follow from a decision, I cannot say this case is allowed or approved by the law of England; and therefore the black must be discharged."

Even so slaves were still sold in London; and by 1788 there were 450,000 slaves in the British West Indies alone. Not until 1807 did England completely abolish the slave trade. The United States in 1794 had passed a law prohibiting American ships or foreign ships clearing American ports from carrying on the slave trade between foreign ports; and in 1807 we forbade the importation of slaves. But, unlike England, we had woven the institution of slavery into the fabric of our law.

When Lincoln first took office in 1861, Negroes who at any time had been slaves could never be citizens; and no descendant of a slave could ever gain citizenship. Even when a slaveowner in the South left a will giving his slaves the choice of returning to Africa or remaining here, the will was not enforced.

For the courts held that a slave had "no legal capacity to elect between freedom and slavery."

In 1857 the Supreme Court ruled in the *Dred Scott* case that even a Negro freed by his owner could not become a citizen of the United States with the right to move from state to state, enjoying all the rights which white men enjoyed. It also ruled that Congress had no power to prevent the spread of slavery into parts of the United States that had not yet become states. Negroes, it was said, were property, and could be taken into any new territory, like cattle or horses, without intervention by Congress. Lincoln thought that decision was wrong and he made many speeches against it. He called the arguments of the judges "sophistical contrivances" which tried to find "some middle ground between the right and the wrong."

On June 16, 1858, he denounced the *Dred Scott* decision in these words:

"Such a decision is all that slavery now lacks of being alike lawful in all the States.

"Welcome or unwelcome, such decision *is* probably coming, and will soon be upon us, unless the power of the present political dynasty shall be met and overthrown.

"We shall *lie down* pleasantly dreaming that the people of *Missouri* are on the verge of making their State *free;* and we shall *awake* to the *reality,* instead, that the *Supreme* Court has made *Illinois* a *slave* State."

THE LONG ROAD TO EQUALITY

Some people said that there was "a line drawn by the Almighty across this continent, on the one side of which the soil must always be cultivated by slaves." He replied:

"If A. can prove, however conclusively, that he may, of right, enslave B.—why may not B. snatch the same argument, and prove equally, that he may enslave A?—

"You say A. is white, and B. is black. It is *color* then; the lighter, having the right to enslave the darker? Take care. By this rule, you are to be slave to the first man you meet, with a fairer skin than your own.

"You do not mean *color* exactly?—You mean the whites are intellectually the superiors of the blacks, and, therefore have the right to enslave them? Take care again. By this rule, you are to be slave to the first man you meet, with an intellect superior to your own."

In 1859, Lincoln told how slavery was ". . . blowing out the moral lights around us; teaching that the negro is no longer a man but a brute; . . . that he ranks with the crocodile and the reptile; that man, with body and soul, is a matter of dollars and cents."

Lincoln knew about slavery first hand. When he had served in Congress, slaves were held in the District of Columbia. There he saw a ". . . sort of Negro-livery stable, where droves of negroes were collected, temporarily kept, and finally taken to Southern markets, precisely like droves of horses."

Negroes were indeed "bought and sold within the sight of the National Capital"—a practice which, in his words, was ". . . offensive in the nostrils of all good men, Southerners as well as Northerners."

As early as 1841 he had traveled the Mississippi: ". . . a fine example was presented on board the boat for contemplating the effect of *condition* upon human happiness. A gentleman had purchased twelve negroes in different parts of Kentucky and was taking them to a farm in the South. They were chained six and six together. A small iron clevis was around the left wrist of each, and this fastened to the main chain by a shorter one at a convenient distance from the others; so that the negroes were strung together precisely like so many fish upon a trot-line. In this condition they were being separated forever from the scenes of their childhood, their friends, their fathers and mothers, and brothers and sisters, and many of them, from their wives and children, and going into perpetual slavery where the lash of the master is proverbially more ruthless and unrelenting than any other. . . ."

He referred to that sight on the boat as "a continual torment to me. . . ." He said that "slave-breeders and slave-traders" were "a small, odious and detested class who made their fortunes out of other people's misery." A man who bought and sold slaves was a "sneaky individual" whom people despised. Years later he said, "If slavery is not wrong, nothing is wrong. I can not remember when I did not so think, and feel."

Many Americans, however, defended slavery.

Stephen A. Douglas, who defeated him for the U.S. Senate in 1858, stated in the campaign: ". . . this government was established on the white basis. It was made by white men, for the benefit of white men and their posterity forever, and never should be administered by any except white men."

Chief Justice Taney of the United States Supreme Court said in the *Dred Scott* case that the words of the Declaration "would seem to embrace the whole human family, and if they were used in a similar instrument at this day would be so understood. But it is too clear for dispute, that the enslaved African race were not intended to be included, and formed no part of the people who framed and adopted this declaration; for if the language, as understood in that day, would embrace them, the conduct of the distinguished men who framed the Declaration of Independence would have been utterly and flagrantly inconsistent with the principles they asserted; and instead of the sympathy of mankind, to which they so confidently appealed, they would have deserved and received universal rebuke and reprobation."

John C. Calhoun had espoused that cause:

". . . I turn to the political; and here I fearlessly assert that the existing relation between the two races in the South, against which these blind fanatics are waging war, forms the most solid and durable foundation on which to rear free and stable political institutions. It is useless to disguise the fact. There is and always has been in an advanced stage of wealth and civilization, a conflict between labor and capital. The condition of society in the South exempts us from the disorders and dangers resulting from this conflict; and which explains why it is that the political condition of the slave-holding States has been so much more stable and quiet than that of the North. The advantages of the former, in this respect, will become more and more manifest if left undisturbed by interference from without, as the country advances in wealth and numbers."

Professor Thomas R. Dew of William and Mary College debated in favor of slavery in 1832. He argued that it is "infinitely more productive" than a society of freemen. Negroes were savages, Dew said; and savages "have been found to be idle and unproductive—except in the chase." The professor added:

"There is nothing but slavery which can destroy those habits of indolence and sloth, and eradicate the character of improvidence and carelessness which mark the independent savage. He may truly be compared to the wild beast of the forest—he must be broke and tamed before he becomes fit for labor and for the task of rearing and providing for a family. There is nothing but slavery which can effect this— the means may appear exceedingly harsh and cruel —and, as among wild beasts many may die in the process of taming and subjugating, so among savages many may not be able to stand the hardships of

servitude; but in the end, it leads on to a milder and
infinitely better condition than that of savage independence, gives rise to greater production, increases
the provisions in nature's great storehouse, and in-
vites into existence a more numerous population,
better fed and better provided; and thus gives rise
to society, and consequently speeds on more rapidly
the cause of civilization."

A Negro minister in Washington, D.C., who was
not educated, answered these educated men:

"How many men can I count in this congregation
who are supporting the families of their white masters with the wages of their labor, besides taking care
of their own wives and children? I am doing it, for
one, and I do not know of any income which my
master has had for a long time except the earnings
of his slaves. If we support ourselves and our masters while we are slaves, we can surely take care of
ourselves when we are free.

"Brethren, the great God has been very kind and
merciful to us and our generation. Just like as He
saved Moses from the crocodiles, and raised him up
to lead his people out of the land of Egypt and out
of the house of bondage; just like as He saved the
dear Lord from the butchers of old wicked Herod,
and bred him up to give every sinful black or white
man or woman one chance to repent and escape out
of the hands of old Satan, so He has now raised up
Mr. Lincoln, and preserved his life, so that he might
give us freedom."

The new President never condemned the Southerners. Those alive in the mid-nineteenth century had not introduced slavery. They had inherited it from their ancestors. Those who lived in the North were not, in his view, more virtuous than those who lived in the South. The Southern people, he said, were just what others would be in their situation. "If slavery did not now exist amongst them, they would not introduce it. If it did now exist amongst us, we should not instantly give it up. . . . This I believe of the masses north and south. . . . We know that some southern men do free their slaves, go north, and become tip-top abolitionists; while some northern ones go south and become most cruel slavemasters."

He realized that, though the immediate cause of the war was not the effort of the North to abolish slavery, slavery must eventually be eliminated because of its immoral character.

The holding of slaves was, indeed, a "peculiar and powerful interest." Once Lincoln had said:

"Those who own them [slaves] look upon them as property, and nothing else. They contemplate them as property, and speak of them as such. The slaves have the same 'property quality,' in the minds of their owners, as any other property. The entire value of the slave population of the United States, is, at a moderate estimate, not less than $2,000,000,000. This amount of *property* has a vast influence upon the minds of those who own it. The same amount of property owned by Northern men has the same influence upon *their* minds. In this we do not assume that we are better than the people of the South— neither do we admit that they are better than we. We are not better, barring circumstances, than they. Public opinion is formed relative to a property basis. Therefore, the slaveholders battle any policy which depreciates their slaves as property. What increases the value of this property, they favor. When you tell them that slavery is immoral, they rebel, because they do not like to be told they are interested in an institution which is not a moral one."

Lincoln's first proposal was to pay the owners of slaves the full value if they would free the slaves. Years ago in Congress, he had introduced a bill to pay owners of slaves in the District of Columbia if they would free them. This proposal received little support. When he became President, he recommended to Congress that it pass a joint resolution proclaiming that the federal government would "co-operate with any state which may adopt gradual abolishment of slavery, giving to such state pecuniary aid" to be used "to compensate for the inconveniences public and private, produced by such change of system." He told Congress that anyone who read the census reports and the Treasury reports would very soon see how "the current expenditures of this war would purchase, at fair valuation, all the slaves in any named State."

Congress accepted his proposal and passed a joint

resolution stating that it favored compensated emancipation. This was in 1862. But no slaveowners offered to free their slaves in exchange for money; and
the war continued unabated.

In the same year he approved an Act of Congress
abolishing slavery in the District of Columbia, paying the owners compensation, and appropriating
money to help Negroes resettle here or abroad. He
said of this measure, "I am gratified that the two
principles of compensation, and colonization, are
both recognized, and practically applied in the act."

He then appealed to the Border States (Delaware,
Kentucky, Maryland, Missouri, and West Virginia)
to adopt programs for compensated emancipation:

"To the people of those states I now earnestly
appeal. I do not argue. I beseech you to make the
arguments for yourselves. You can not, if you would,
be blind to the signs of the times. I beg of you a
calm and enlarged consideration of them, ranging, if
it may be, far above personal and partisan politics.
This proposal makes common cause for a common
object, casting no reproaches upon any. It acts not
the Pharisee. The change it contemplates would
come gently as the dews of heaven, not rending or
wrecking anything. Will you not embrace it? So
much good has not been done, by one effort, in all
past time, as, in the providence of God, it is now
your high privilege to do. May the vast future not
have lament that you have neglected it."

He decided to press for compensated emancipation

in Delaware. It was after all the smallest slaveowning state and had the fewest slaves. He thought that if Delaware would adopt the plan the other Border States would follow. Throughout 1862 his political followers in Delaware promoted the idea. But the state officials elected that year were opposed.

Lincoln pleaded with the Congressmen and Senators from the Border States to support his program for compensated emancipation. As to the expense involved he cited a few figures. If the slaves in Delaware were freed at $400 each, it would cost $719,000. This was an insignificant amount, he pointed out, because the war cost two million dollars per day. By his computations all of the slaves in the Border States and in the District of Columbia could be purchased for what eighty-seven days of war would cost. He emphasized that, if the war continued, slavery would be extinguished forcibly without any payment for the slaves:

"How much better for you, and for your people, to take the step which, at once, shortens the war, and secures substantial compensation for that which is sure to be wholly lost in any other event. How much better to thus save the money which else we sink forever in the war. How much better to do it while we can, lest the war ere long render us pecuniarily unable to do it. How much better for you, as seller, and the nation as buyer, to sell out, and buy out, that without which the war could never have been, than to sink both the thing to be sold, and the price of it, in cutting one another's throats.

"I do not speak of emancipation *at once*, but of a *decision* at once to emancipate *gradually*. Room in South America for colonization, can be obtained cheaply, and in abundance; and when numbers shall be large enough to be company and encouragement for one another, the freed people will not be so reluctant to go."

But the Congressional Delegation from the Border States, after considering the proposal, rejected it— twenty members voting against it, and only eight being in favor.

Thereupon he sent a message to Congress recommending a constitutional amendment which would provide for compensation to owners of slaves in states which abolished slavery before the year 1900:

"The emancipation will be unsatisfactory to the advocates of perpetual slavery; but the length of time should greatly mitigate their dissatisfaction. The time spares both races from the evils of sudden derangement—in fact, from the necessity of any derangement—while most of those whose habitual course of thought will be disturbed by the measure will have passed away before its consummation. They will never see it. Another class will hail the prospect of emancipation, but will deprecate the length of time. They will feel that it gives too little to the now living slaves. But it really gives them much. It saves them from the vagrant destitution which must largely attend immediate emancipation in localities where their numbers are very great; and it gives the inspiring assurance that their posterity shall be free forever. The plan leaves to each state, choosing to act under it, to abolish slavery now, or at the end of the century, or at any intermediate time, or by degrees, extending over the whole or any part of the period; and it obliges no two states to proceed alike."

He gave two reasons for compensating the slaveowners. First, he thought payment of money would induce the owners to give up their slaves. Secondly, he said:

"In a certain sense the liberation of slaves is the destruction of property—property acquired by descent, or by purchase, the same as any other property. It is no less true for having been often said, that the people of the south are not more responsible for the original introduction of this property, than are the people of the north; and when it is remembered how unhesitatingly we all use cotton and sugar, and share the profits of dealing in them, it may not be quite safe to say, that the south has been more responsible than the north for its continuance. If then, for a common object, this property is to be sacrificed is it not just that it be done at a common charge?"

Bills introduced in Congress to carry his recommendations into effect met resistance. One indignant Congressman said: "The people of my district will not permit themselves to be taxed to purchase Negroes while the wives and children of our gallant soldiers are starving."

Though one bill passed the House and another the Senate, the two houses for one reason or another never agreed upon a bill.

Slavery was indeed a "peculiar and powerful interest" as evidenced by the way in which the owners hung tenaciously to their slaves. The idea of being paid, if they would set their slaves free, was as repulsive to the owners as it was to those who shook their fists at slaveowners and called them criminals. The passions that gathered around that issue clouded and confused all discussion of it.

The idea persisted that Negroes were members of an "inferior" race and that they should be treated only with as much allowance as they were capable of enjoying.

Lincoln replied that those were the arguments "that kings have made for enslaving the people of all ages of the world . . . that all the arguments in favor of king-craft were of this class. . . ." He said that kings "always bestrode the necks of the people not that they wanted to do it, but because the people were better off for being ridden."

He compared slavery with the "Divine Right of Kings":

"By the latter, the King is to do just as he pleases with his white subjects, being responsible to God alone. By the former the white man is to do just as he pleases with his black slaves, being responsible to God alone. The two things are precisely alike; and it is but natural that they should find similar arguments to sustain them."

The conflict over slavery did not have its origins in America; it was deep in human history:

"It is the eternal struggle between these two principles—right and wrong—throughout the world. They are the two principles that have stood face to face from the beginning of time; and will ever continue to struggle. The one is the common right of humanity and the other the divine right of kings. It is the same principle in whatever shape it develops itself. It is the same spirit that says, 'You work and toil and earn bread, and I'll eat it.' No matter in what shape it comes, whether from the mouth of a king who seeks to bestride the people of his own nation and live by the fruit of their labor, or from one race of men as an apology for enslaving another race, it is the same tyrannical principle."

The slaves, about "one-eighth of the whole population" as he described them, or 12½ percent, were owned by about 350,000 families. Those families were composed of 1,750,000 people. The national population was about 37 million. That meant that the "peculiar and powerful interest" concerned with ownership of the 12½ percent was really less than 5 percent of the people in the United States.

"One-eighth of the whole population were colored slaves, not distributed generally over the Union, but localized in the Southern part of it. These slaves constituted a peculiar and powerful interest. All knew that this interest was, somehow, the cause of the war. To strengthen, perpetuate, and extend this interest was the object for which the insurgents would rend the Union, even by war; while the government claimed no right to do more than to restrict the territorial enlargement of it.

Neither party expected for the war the magnitude or the duration which it has already attained. Neither anticipated that the *cause* of the conflict might cease with, or even before, the conflict itself should cease. Each looked for an easier triumph, and a result less fundamental and astounding."

# FOUR

L INCOLN, A DEEPLY RELIGIOUS MAN, HAD CONFIDENCE
that "the God of Nations" would sustain the
human rights involved in the Civil War. His religion
sustained his belief that man should be God's instrument to remove the curse of slavery from the nation.

Fathers and mothers in the South, like fathers and
mothers in the North, prayed for the safety of their
sons, for the end of war, for victory for their side.

Jefferson Davis, President of the Confederacy, also
prayed to God. He declared in 1863 that "the proper
condition of the negro is slavery"—"a complete sub-
jugation to the white man." He believed that slavery
was ordained "by decree of Almighty God." He believed that God had created the black man unequal
to the white man in every and all cases and for every
and all purposes.

Jefferson Davis, defending slavery before the Civil
War, denounced people who said slavery was a "sin."
Davis asked, "Who gave them the right to decide
that it is a sin? By what standard do they measure
it? . . . Not the Bible; that justifies it. Not the good
of Society; for if they go where it exists, they find

that society recognizes it as good." He went on to state that Christianity was not opposed to slavery, for in his views, "servitude is the only agency through which Christianity has reached that degraded race."

To prove that the Bible was behind slavery Davis argued:

"When Cain, for the commission of the first great crime, was driven from the face of Adam, no longer the fit associate of those who were created to exercise dominion over the earth, he found in the land of Nod those to whom his crime had degraded him to an equality; and when the low and vulgar son of Noah, who laughed at his father's exposure, sunk by debasing himself and his lineage by a connection with an inferior race of men, he doomed his descendants to perpetual slavery. Noah spoke the decree, or prophecy, as gentlemen may choose to consider it, one or the other."

When people maintained that slavery was sanctioned by the Bible, the man who was to lead the North against Jefferson Davis pointed out that the slavery described in the Bible was "the slavery of the white man—of men without reference to color." Lincoln was right, because the slaves in Biblical days included men of all races captured in war, as well as Negroes kidnaped in Africa. And he went on to show that, if making one man a slave was proper, any man could be made a slave.

His creed held that every man has dignity, every man a spark of the divine. All men should stand equally before the law and before God. That was what the teachings of the Bible meant to him. His prayers were for humanity, for freedom, for the equality of all men regardless of race, creed, or color.

Many slaves fled north to gain their freedom, and often their masters went in pursuit of them. Fugitive slave laws were in force which permitted slaveowners to get northern courts to direct a return of their slaves.

In 1858 John Brown raided Missouri, freed twelve slaves, and escorted them to freedom in Canada. The success of that raid inspired many other slaves to escape. A year later, Brown, whose idea was to cause the slaves to revolt against their masters, seized Harpers Ferry, a government arsenal, with a view toward encouraging slaves to take to the hills and gain their freedom. This time, Brown was captured and tried for creating rebellion against Virginia. John Brown contended that what he had done "in behalf of His despised poor, is no wrong, but right." He was found guilty and hanged.

The escape of slaves continued, and John Brown, dead, became a more potent influence than John Brown, alive. He became a symbol of emancipation: "John Brown's body lies a-mouldering in the grave, but his soul goes marching on."

Northern sympathizers formed "underground railroads" to help the slaves escape from the South. Those "underground railroads" extended from Kansas and Nebraska in the west to Massachusetts in the east. People in the North hid the runaway slaves in the daytime and helped them travel at night. They were passed on from town to town. Hundreds upon hundreds of slaves moved north, their destination Canada. Once they reached Canada there was no fugitive slave law through which their masters could reclaim them.

As the Union armies captured slaveowning areas, the Negroes flocked in vast numbers into the camps of the Yankees. Congress had by now provided that all fugitives reaching the Union lines would be free. Slaves becoming soldiers in the Union armies were also freed. The Negro encampments alongside Union armies grew and grew. It was estimated that fifty thousand slaves joined Grant after the battle of Chattanooga.

The Union Army established special units to take care of these Negro refugees. These Negroes were in desperate condition, needing food, shelter, medicines. Contagious diseases spread fast among them, causing many deaths. There were no doctors available, and no hospitals. Those who were able-bodied were put to work for the government as laborers and paid wages. None were "forced into the service." If work for private persons was found and Negro refugees assigned to it, the private employer was expected to pay the going wages.

Sometimes the Negroes following a Union army exceeded the size of the army. At times the problem of taking care of these Negro refugees was greater than that of providing for the army itself.

By an act of July 17, 1862, the President was authorized to enroll Negroes in the Army or Navy either as soldiers, sailors, or laborers. While some Negroes were used in military service in 1862, recruiting did not take place on an organized basis until the spring of 1863. In all, nearly 200,000 Negroes fought for the Union Army in the war, over half of whom were recruited in the South.

A northern state could fill its quota for the Army by going into Confederate territory, enlisting Negroes, taking them north, and putting them into the armed services. Agents for states often competed against each other in such projects, offering southern Negroes as much as $500 to join their Army.

Prior to the Emancipation Proclamation the Union Army had used Negroes mostly as laborers. Shortly afterward, Colonel T. W. Higginson of Massachusetts took command of a slave regiment made up of volunteers from South Carolina. He trained them and took them on several raids. Colonel R. A. Shaw of Massachusetts also organized a colored regiment. Colonel Shaw and half of his recruits were soon killed in battle. A statue of Colonel Shaw, executed by St. Gaudens, stands today on the Boston Common. But when he marched his colored troops out of Boston, many of its citizens were not proud. They drew their blinds rather than watch the sight. Later, William James said that what Shaw and his comrades showed was that in an emergency "Americans of all complexions and conditions can go forth like brothers, and meet death cheerfully if need be, in order that this religion of our native land—that a man requires no master—shall not become a failure on the earth."

By early 1863 four colored regiments were operating. By August, 1864, there were about 150,000 colored troops in the Union Army. Before war's end they saw much action. The President, who in the beginning had not contemplated the use of colored troops, spoke of them shortly after the Emancipation Proclamation as "very important, if not indispensable." On March 26, 1863, he wrote Andrew Johnson, who had become Governor of Tennessee once it was freed of Confederates:

"I am told you have at least *thought* of raising a negro military force. In my opinion the country now needs no specific thing so much as some man of your ability, and position, to go to this work. When I speak of your position, I mean that of an eminent citizen of a slave-state, and himself a slave-holder. The colored population is the great *available,* and yet *unavailed* of, force for restoring the Union. The bare sight of fifty thousand armed, and drilled black soldiers on the banks of the Mississippi, would end the rebellion at once. And who doubts that we can present that sight, if we but take hold in earnest?"

By the act of February 24, 1864, "all able-bodied male colored persons" between the ages of twenty and forty-five were drafted for military service. This law covered Negroes who were slaves as well as Negroes who were free. Slaveowners in the Border States, which had not seceded, violently objected to the taking of their slaves without compensation. "What right have you to insist that our slaves in Kentucky be drafted?" People from Delaware, Maryland, and Missouri also asked that question. So the act provided that when a slave was taken into the Army from the Border States, his master should receive a sum of money (from $100 to $300) and the slave should become a free man.

On February 7, 1865, the President wrote a commanding officer in Kentucky, "Complaint is made to me that you are forcing negroes into the military service, and even torturing them—riding them on rails and the like—to extort their consent. I hope this may be a mistake. The like must not be done by you, or any one under you. You must not force negroes any more than white men."

The use of Negro troops by the Union Army inflamed the South. On April 30, 1863, the Confederate Congress passed a law that white officers commanding Negro troops should be "deemed as making servile insurrection" and, if captured, "put to death or be otherwise punished."

The President on July 30, 1863, proclaimed that for every Union soldier so killed "a rebel soldier shall be executed" and for every one enslaved "a rebel shall be placed at hard labor."

At Fort Pillow, Tennessee, garrisoned by Negro troops, a bloody incident occurred on April 12, 1864.

Confederate soldiers took it and at least three hundred Negro soldiers were killed. The North said it was a brutal "massacre." The South said the Negroes were killed in combat. The President acted with restraint. Whatever may have been the truth of the charges, he did not retaliate. For in his view retaliation would have only made matters worse.

By late 1864 the South was having difficulty getting men for its armies. Negroes in the Confederate Army were used for many tasks but not for the actual firing of guns. Conscription of white men was rigorous. All white males between the ages of eighteen and thirty-five were called in April, 1862. In September, 1862, those between thirty-five and forty-five were added. By February, 1864, all between seventeen and fifty had been conscripted. In 1864 there was talk in the South about putting slaves in the Army. Judah P. Benjamin, Secretary of State of the Confederacy, said, "Let us say to every Negro who wishes to go into the ranks on the condition of being made free: 'Go and fight and you are free.'" General Lee on January 11, 1865, announced in favor of it, saying that all slaves who enlisted should be given "immediate freedom" and that their families should be given their freedom at the end of the war as a reward for faithful discharge of military duties. Lee went further and recommended that this measure be accompanied by "a well-digested plan of gradual and general emancipation."

When the President heard that the Confederacy

was attempting to persuade Negro slaves to join the armies of the South, he said:

". . . If he shall now really fight to keep himself a slave, it will be a far better argument why [he] should remain a slave than I have ever before heard. He, perhaps, ought to be a slave, if he desires it ardently enough to fight for it. Or, if one out of four will, for his own freedom, fight to keep the other three in slavery, he ought to be a slave for his selfish meanness. I have always thought that all men should be free; but if any should be slaves it should be first those who desire it for *themselves,* and secondly those who *desire* it for *others.*"

The enlistment of slaves by the armies of the South met opposition. The view stated by one slaveowner at the beginning of the war was the view of most slaveowners at the end of the war: "The day you make soldiers of them [the Negroes] is the beginning of the end of the revolution. If slaves will make good soldiers, our whole theory of slavery is wrong."

Yet by 1864 and 1865 the South, very anxious for recognition as a separate nation by European powers, was representing abroad that she planned emancipation. Because of Lincoln's astute management of the situation, by the end of 1864 and the beginning of 1865 defense of slavery as an institution was disappearing even in the South.

Once the Negroes were trained as soldiers, they fought well. Some Union officers thought Negro soldiers had more to fight for than the others. As one officer said, "They fought with ropes around their necks." More than thirty-eight thousand Negro soldiers lost their lives in the Civil War.

". . . Both read the same Bible, and pray to the same God; and each invokes His aid against the other. It may seem strange that any men should dare to ask a just God's assistance in wringing their bread from the sweat of other men's faces; but let us judge not, that we be not judged. The prayers of both could not be answered—that of neither has been answered fully."

# FIVE

ONE OF LINCOLN'S MAIN EFFORTS WAS TO
keep the Border States (Delaware, Kentucky,
Maryland, Missouri, and West Virginia) from join-
ing the Confederacy, a plan that had unexpected
consequences.

During the year 1861 much blood was spilled in
Missouri when 5,000 Northern troops met 11,000
Confederates in battle. There was so much loss of
life that he expressed the hope that the conflict would
not "degenerate into a violent and remorseless revo-
lutionary struggle."

Missouri in 1861 was part slave, part free. In St.
Louis and vicinity the Northern Army took over the
government. The Confederates marched on Jefferson
City, the capital. In August, 1861, the two armies
joined in battle at Wilson's Creek. The casualties
were severe, about equal on each side. General John
Charles Frémont, who commanded the Northern
Army, issued a proclamation. Under the proclamation, if anyone either took up arms against the
United States or took "an active part" with the Confederates, his property would be confiscated and his

slaves would be "declared freemen." Frémont also drew a line across Missouri and declared that all persons caught north of the line "with arms in their hands" would be court-martialed and shot. Frémont issued the proclamation without consulting the President.

The President, who was opposed to slavery, was also opposed to Frémont's proclamation. He wrote a friend on September 22, 1861: "General Frémont's proclamation, as to confiscation of property, and the liberation of slaves, is *purely political,* and not within the range of *military* law, or necessity. If a commanding General finds a necessity to seize the farm of a private owner, for a pasture, an encampment, or a fortification, he has the right to do so, and to so hold it, as long as the necessity lasts; and this is within military law, because within military necessity. But to say the farm shall no longer belong to the owner, or his heirs forever; and this as well when the farm is not needed for military purposes as when it is, is purely political, without the savor of military law about it. And the same is true of slaves. If the General needs them, he can seize them, and use them; but when the need is past, it is not for him to fix their permanent future condition. That must be settled according to laws made by law-makers, and not by military proclamations. The proclamation in the point in question, is simply 'dictatorship.' It assumes that the general may do *anything* he pleases—confiscate the lands and free the slaves of *loyal* people, as

well as of disloyal ones. And going the whole figure
I have no doubt would be more popular with some
thoughtless people, than that which has been done!
But I cannot assume this reckless position; nor allow
others to assume it on my responsibility."

At this point in the war he was hoping to avoid the
forcible abolition of slavery. He was looking for a
victory against the seceding states; and, as a means to
that end, he sought to keep the Border States in the
Union.

He therefore asked Frémont to modify the proclamation, saying that "the confiscation of property and
the liberation of slaves of traitorous owners will
alarm our Southern Union friends and turn them
against us; perhaps ruin our rather fair prospect for
Kentucky." When Frémont refused, he modified it.

He was criticized by the antislavery people for
doing this. Why not seize on every opportunity to
free the slaves? they asked. He, however, had a longer
view. While he was against slavery, his immediate
aim was to win the war. Kentucky seemed to be
teetering. Would she secede? Soldiers in Kentucky,
hearing of Frémont's proclamation, threw down their
arms and refused to defend the Union cause. He
feared that if the Union lost Kentucky, the four
other Border States might also be lost. If Maryland
seceded, he thought it would be just as well to surrender Washington, D.C., because the nation's capital would then be encircled by Maryland on the
north, and by Virginia on the south. That is why he

wrote, "I think to lose Kentucky is nearly the same as to lose the whole game."

He feared that if Frémont shot people in Missouri for having guns in their hands, the Confederates would "shoot as many of our men." His fears were justified, for the Confederate general in charge of southern Missouri issued a proclamation that matched Frémont's—for every soldier put to death by Frémont he would "hang, draw, and quarter a minion of said Abraham Lincoln."

Before many weeks passed he removed Frémont over the protests of many slavery people. Even Horace Greeley, the famous New York editor who had been instrumental in nominating him in 1860, protested. Greeley, in 1861, on his support of the President in 1860, was quoted as saying: "It was a mistake—the biggest mistake of my life."

On May 9, 1862, a Union general, David Hunter, freed the slaves in Georgia, Florida, and South Carolina. Prior thereto, Congress had passed the joint resolution agreeing to give financial assistance to any state which adopted a gradual abolishment of slavery. The President thought that what General Hunter did was inconsistent with that action of Congress. On May 19, 1862, he declared Hunter's order to be "altogether void." The question of declaring slaves free "I reserve to myself." He deemed that decision inappropriate for "commanders in the field."

In his view General Ulysses S. Grant acted more properly in Kentucky than Frémont had done in

Missouri and Hunter in Georgia, Florida, and South Carolina. Early in 1862 Grant moved 18,000 troops down the Mississippi on gunboats from St. Louis. They turned up the Ohio River and then via the Tennessee River into Kentucky. They disembarked and marched cross-country to engage the Confederates at Fort Donelson on the Cumberland River that runs parallel to the Tennessee and empties into the Ohio. In a short while the Confederates surrendered, Grant taking over 13,000 prisoners. Several months prior to that victory, Grant had issued a proclamation to the Kentuckians:

"I have come among you, not as an enemy, but as your friend and fellow citizen, not to injure or annoy you, but to respect the rights, and to defend and enforce the rights of all loyal citizens. . . . I have nothing to do with opinions. I shall deal only with armed rebellion and its aiders and abettors. . . ."

That was the President's attitude toward the South in 1862. He still "looked for a result" less fundamental and astounding than the abolition of slavery without compensating the owners. He praised Grant's proclamation: "The modesty and brevity of that address show that the officer issuing it understands the situation, and is the proper man to command there at this time."

Greeley had become so dissatisfied with the President's leadership that on August 19, 1862, he published his views in an open letter entitled "The Prayer of Twenty Millions."

*49*

Greeley complained that the President was treating the southern "traitors" too tenderly. He said that the man in the White House, by dealing softly with the Border States, where slavery sentiment was strong, strengthened "treason and drives home the wedge intended to divide the Union." He denounced the President for not having abolished slavery. He said, "We have fought wolves with the devices of sheep." He insisted that ". . . every hour of deference to slavery is an hour of added and deepened peril to the Union." He chastised the Commander in Chief for annulling the proclamations issued by Frémont and Hunter. He ended by saying, "We must have scouts, guides, spies, cooks, teamsters, diggers and choppers from the blacks of the South, whether we allow them to fight for us or not, or we shall be baffled and repelled."

The President replied:

"I would save the Union. I would save it the shortest way under the Constitution. The sooner the National authority can be restored, the nearer the Union will be 'the Union as it was.' If there be those who would not save the Union, unless they could at the same time *save* Slavery, I do not agree with them. If there be those who would not save the Union unless they could at the same time *destroy* Slavery, I do not agree with them. My paramount object in this struggle *is* to save the Union, and is *not* either to save or to destroy Slavery. If I could save the Union without freeing *any* slave, I would do it, and if I could save it by freeing *all* the slaves, I would do it; and if I could save it by freeing some and leaving others alone, I would also do that. What I do about Slavery, and the colored race, I do because I believe it helps to save this Union; and what I forbear, I forbear because I do *not* believe it would help to save the Union. I shall do *less* whenever I shall believe what I am doing hurts the cause, and do *more* whenever I shall believe doing more will help the cause. I shall try to correct errors when shown to be errors; and I shall adopt new views so fast as they shall appear to be true views.

"I have here stated my purpose according to my view of *official* duty; and I intend no modification of my oft-expressed *personal* wish that all men everywhere could be free."

In 1861 and 1862 the Union armies had not fared too well. He realized that, though the manpower of the South was being drastically cut down by casualties, many battles remained. "It might go on twenty or thirty years, using up a generation of people." This was his concern when the year 1862 was coming to a close. There was also a Congressional election in 1862. The Union armies were not making much progress in the war; and the sentiment against him was growing. The abolitionists thought he was not sufficiently antislavery; those who wanted to crush the South thought he was too lenient; those who expected a quick victory criticized his military tactics.

On September 13, 1862, a Chicago delegation of

"Christians of All Denominations" urged that he emancipate the slaves. He exchanged views with members of the delegation, saying that "as Commander-In-Chief of the army and navy in time of war, I suppose I have a right to take any measure which may best subdue the enemy." His position in short was this:

"I view the matter as a practical war measure, to be decided upon according to the advantages or disadvantages it may offer to the suppression of the rebellion."

On September 22, 1862, he issued a preliminary Emancipation Proclamation stating that on January 1, 1863, he would list the states and parts of states where slaves would be "forever free."

Yet, in spite of this promise, his party, the Republicans, lost heavily in the 1862 Congressional election. It lost even Illinois, his home state. The Republicans had 106 members in Congress from 1860-1862. In 1862 the early election returns showed that they had only 80, while the Democrats had 75. Then came reports from Kentucky, Maryland, Missouri, and West Virginia showing that they had elected Republicans, which increased the majority by 18 votes. But for the Border States, his position in Congress would have been greatly weakened.

After the election he kept the promise he made on September 22, 1862, signing the Emancipation Proclamation on January 1, 1863. It declared that the slaves held in areas described in the Proclamation "are and henceforward shall be free." It freed slaves only in areas under Confederate control. All of Tennessee was excluded; as were Union states where slavery existed. Even portions of Virginia and Tennessee held by the Union Army were excluded.

He urged these emancipated people "to abstain from all violence, unless in necessary self-defense" and to "labor faithfully for reasonable wages." He declared that they would be received into the Armed Forces of the United States.

Jefferson Davis in retaliation declared on January 12, 1863, that all free Negroes thereafter captured and all free Negroes in the South would be made slaves. The Confederate President ordered that northern officers thereafter captured be treated not as prisoners of war but as "criminals engaged in exciting servile insurrection." Davis added that the Proclamation "has established a state of things which can lead to but one of three possible consequences— the extermination of the slaves, the exile of the whole white population from the Confederacy, or absolute and total separation of these States from the United States." Davis ended his statement with the words: "Let us then join in returning thanks to God and in beseeching the continuance of His protecting care over our cause and in the restoration of peace with its manifold blessings to our beloved country."

On January 8, 1863, the President stated in a letter the reasons behind the Emancipation Proclamation:

"After the commencement of hostilities, I struggled nearly a year and a half to get along without touching the 'institution'; and when finally I conditionally determined to touch it, I gave a hundred days fair notice of any purpose, to all the States and people, within which time they could have turned it wholly aside, by simply again becoming good citizens of the United States. They chose to disregard it, and I made the peremptory proclamation on what appeared to me to be a military necessity."

What the President criticized Frémont and Hunter for doing in 1861 and 1862, he himself did on January 1, 1863. It was his political judgment that conditions had sufficiently changed by that time to make emancipation not only desirable but necessary.

He issued the Proclamation as Commander in Chief of the Army and Navy in an effort to weaken the enemy. The Commander in Chief could blockade the ports of the enemy to keep supplies from reaching him. By the same reasoning, he was entitled to weaken the South by freeing its slaves and robbing it of manpower.

In a letter on August 26, 1863, he defended the Emancipation Proclamation:

"I think the Constitution invests its Commander-In-Chief with the law of war, in time of war. The most that can be said, if so much is that slaves are property. Is there . . . has there ever been—any question that by the law of war, property, both of enemies and friends, may be taken when needed?

And is it not needed whenever taking it helps us or hurts the enemy? Armies, the world over, destroy enemies' property when they cannot use it; and even destroy their own to keep it from the enemy."

A Richmond paper called him a fiend and the Proclamation the "fiend's new programme," destroying "four thousand millions of our property" and bidding the slaves "to rise in insurrection." It was construed in the South as an incitement to the slaves to strike against their masters.

The Negroes did not rise against their masters. There were no bloody incidents in the South between whites and blacks as a result of the Emancipation Proclamation.

Though Congress, prior to the Proclamation, had already freed some slaves, the Proclamation dramatized emancipation. Thereafter, "emancipation" became a slogan. People began to think of the war in new terms—as a war against slavery. The Emancipation Proclamation, though in law narrow and confined, became the symbol of a new struggle—the battle to free people from bondage. January 1, 1863, became a famous day in the world's almanac of liberty. In people's imagination it symbolized the time when shackles were removed from the hands and legs of people everywhere in the world.

At the start of the war Lincoln, like others, had rejected the idea of the forcible freeing of slaves. Yet before the war ended he declared tens of thousands of slaves free and paid the owners no compensation. He did this to weaken the South.

The President was once charged with having changed his mind within a short time.

"Yes, I have," he replied. "And I don't think much of a man who is not wiser today than he was yesterday."

By the time the Republicans met in convention in 1864 to select their Presidential candidate, the antislavery sentiment had new support. E. J. More, a lawyer of Allentown, Pennsylvania, who attended that convention, wrote his wife on June 7, 1864, concerning the attitude of the Republican delegates from the Border States where slavery was still in existence:

"One remarkable feature about the delegates from the slave states in attendance here is that they are more intensely in favor of the entire unconditional abolition in the total annihilation of slavery than our most uncompromising anti-slavery men in the North. They utterly abhor and despise the thing and there is an old fellow here from Kentucky who is still the nominal owner of slaves in that state who *swears* that every slave in the land must be made free by constitutional amendment. These men are very evidently becoming as positive and vindictive in their opposition to slavery as they formerly were in its support for they are all men with very strongly marked features."

By late 1864, over one million slaves had won their freedom.

Many forces were at work beckoning the Negro to a new freedom. Some progress in abolition of slavery by the states was being made. West Virginia in 1863 adopted a constitution providing for gradual emancipation. Maryland abolished slavery in 1864. The President on October 10, 1864, wrote a friend in Maryland in support of Maryland's proposal: "I wish all men to be free. I wish the material prosperity of the already free which I feel sure the extinction of slavery would bring. I wish to see, in process of disappearing, that only thing which ever could bring this nation to civil war."

Missouri in 1863 had provided in its constitution that all slaves would be freed July 4, 1870. But those over forty years of age were to remain under the control and subject to the authority of their owners as servants for life; those under twelve years of age until they reached twenty-three; and all others until July 4, 1876.

On July 31, 1863, the President wrote that he would not object to this Missouri plan "on account of the time for *ending* the institution" of slavery. But he expressed the regret that "the *beginning* should have been postponed for seven years, leaving all that time to agitate for the repeal of the whole thing. It should begin at once, giving at least the new-born, a vested interest in freedom, which could not be taken away." But his views for faster progress in Missouri did not immediately prevail.

In 1863 Andrew Johnson as Governor of Ten-

nessee announced he was in favor of the emancipation of slaves. The President congratulated him:

"All Tennessee is now clear of armed insurrec-
tionists. You need not to be reminded that it is the
nick of time for re-inaugurating a loyal State government. Not a moment should be lost. You and the
co-operating friends there, can better judge the ways
and means that can be judged by any here. I only
offer a few suggestions. The re-inauguration must
not be such as to give control of the State, and its
representation in Congress, to the enemies of the
Union, driving its friends there into political exile.
. . . Let the reconstruction be the work of such men
only as can be trusted for the Union. Exclude all
others, and trust that your government, so organized, will be recognized here, as being the one of
republican form, to be guaranteed to the State, and
to be protected against invasion and domestic violence. . . ."

"I see that you have declared in favor of emancipation in Tennessee, for which, may God bless you.
Get emancipation into your new . . . constitution. . . ."

The final abolition of slavery was not, however,
achieved in Tennessee until February, 1865.

Meanwhile the political pressures for abolition increased in the North. If slavery was to be abolished
soon, the central government must act.

In 1864 a resolution was introduced in the Congress to submit to the states an amendment to the

Constitution abolishing slavery. No compensation to slaveowners was provided. On that ground some protested, saying that it was unjust "to seize this property" without any payment to owners, many of whom were still loyal to the Union. April 8, 1864, the Senate passed the resolution by a vote of 38 to 6, that being the necessary two-thirds vote required by the Constitution for a Constitutional amendment. The resolution had more opposition in the House. Its proponents denounced "the bogus aristocracy of slavery," and the evils and bloodshed which "this demon of slavery" brought to this nation. They thought that "we can have no permanent peace while slavery lives." They maintained that abolition would weaken the South and strengthen the armies of the North.

Those opposed to the resolution were generally of two schools of thought. Eleven states, parties to the Constitution, were not represented in this Congress. Some Congressmen, therefore, thought that the remaining states should not make "a fundamental change in Government" that would overturn the social and industrial systems of the absent states. Others thought abolition of slavery should come from the states, not from the federal government. The vote in the House on June 15, 1864, was only 93 for the resolution while 65 were against it and 23 did not vote. It, therefore, did not pass, since it lacked the two-thirds vote.

After the 1864 election and before the Second Inaugural, the President sent a message to Congress urging reconsideration of the resolution. The election showed, he said, "almost certainly that the next Congress will pass the measure if this does not."

The opposition to abolition in Congress was still strong. Some said there are "causes at work, which in any event" will destroy slavery. It was also pointed out that, when the Constitution went into operation, the slave states outnumbered the free states, putting it within their power to "force slavery on Massachusetts, in the same way you propose to force abolition on the South. Would Massachusetts . . . have submitted to so gross a perversion of the compact she had just entered into?" Others feared the prospect of free Negroes working side by side with "the native and foreign-born white laborers of the North." It was said, "We may as well expect the most opposite in nature to be reconciled, the most incongruous to harmonize, as that such a thing can happen. No need but to take one step further to advocate amalgamation. I hope . . . that this hitherto glorious and happy country, the home and asylum of millions of white men, will not be doomed to become the land of a race of hybrids, and thus by degrees be blotted out of existence in accordance with the immutable laws of nature."

On January 31, 1865, the House took another vote and passed the resolution by the necessary two-thirds majority, 119 voting for it, 56 voting against it, and 8 not voting.

Lincoln's policy toward the Border States had paid large dividends. Of the Senators from those states only those from Delaware and Kentucky had voted against the resolution. Of the Congressmen from the Border States only one (a Missourian) stood opposed to it.

Thus there was sent to the states for consideration the Thirteenth Amendment, which reads:

"Neither slavery nor involuntary servitude, except as a punishment for crime whereof the party shall have been duly convicted, shall exist within the United States, or any place subject to their jurisdiction."

That Amendment (ratified December 18, 1865) set nearly four million slaves free. The President still believed in compensating slaveowners when their slaves were made free.

In spite of the fact that the Thirteenth Amendment had been approved by the Congress and was being considered by the states, in spite of the fact that it seemed likely that the states would adopt it, he presented to his Cabinet a proposal that Congress provide for compensation to the slaveowning states on certain conditions. His idea was to pay $400 million to those states—half to be paid if the states ended all resistance by April 1, 1865, the other half to be paid if the states adopted the Thirteenth Amendment by July 1, 1865.

He predicted that, if these things were done, the "war will cease" and armies will be "reduced to a basis of peace," that "all political offenses will be pardoned," that "all property, except slaves, liable to confiscation or forfeiture, will be released" with certain exceptions, and that "liberality will be recommended to Congress upon all points not lying within executive control."

His idea was to promote the cause of peace by paying what he estimated to be the expense of conducting the war for another two hundred days. The Cabinet debated this proposal and rejected it. One Cabinet officer, Gideon Welles, summed up their feelings: "In the present temper of Congress the proposed measure, if a wise one, could not be carried through successfully."

The President rejoiced, of course, over the Thirteenth Amendment. He said that it was "a King's cure for all evils. It winds the whole thing up." It was in his view the "indispensable adjunct to the consummation of the great game we are playing." He was particularly pleased that Illinois, his home state, was the first to approve the Thirteenth Amendment.

As long as there was slavery there would be a deep division in the nation that would make for discord and conflict—a line drawn between "the love of property" on the one side and "a consciousness of right and wrong" on the other.

He knew that until the mass of people who were held as slaves had been freed and admitted to first-class citizenship America would never speak with one voice.

He himself was a product of adversity. His sympathies were naturally with the underdog, the man striving for a place in the sun. He had confidence that the Negroes would be citizens worthy of American ideals. He put this confidence in words that all could understand: "No men living are more worthy to be trusted than those who toil up from poverty."

The threats to America's existence, he claimed, did not come from abroad. They were, in his views, threats generated from forces of injustice working within the nation. "If destruction be our lot," he said, "we must ourselves be its author and finisher. As a nation of freemen, we must live through all time, or die by suicide."

Abolition of slavery removed a cancer from society. Only when all cells of that cancer had disappeared would the nation be well and healthy. Social injustices had destroyed nations from within since the beginning of civilization. Discrimination against minorities set up a process of decay. Countries became weak when they were divided. They became weak when people distrusted each other.

Two hundred and fifty years of slavery were two hundred and fifty years too many. The poison of discrimination had entered the bloodstream of the nation and sapped its strength. Only when all men toiled equally, only when opportunities were open to everyone, only when men of lowly birth, the sons of illiterate slaves, were in law on the same political plane as the sons of the aristocracy would the nation be strong in body and soul.

"The Almighty has His own purposes. Woe unto the world because of offenses! for it must needs be that offenses come; but woe to that man by whom the offense cometh!"

CHAPTER

# SIX

W ERE THE "REBELS" SINNERS WHO HAD TO BE
punished? Should they be forgiven for past
actions and welcomed back into the American family once they indicated their loyalty to the national
government? In order to re-enter the Union would
they have to admit Negroes to full voting rights?
Could there be a period of transition so that ex-slaves
might be educated and better prepared for citizenship? If Negroes in the South were to be allowed to
vote, should Negroes up North be given the same
rights? Some northern states did not let Negroes vote.
Who then were they to sit in judgment on Southerners who did the same?

In 1863 a critical struggle between the White
House and the Hill over these issues began to take
shape. Much "rebel" territory had been conquered
and was under northern rule. Due largely to the efforts of General Ulysses S. Grant and Admiral D. G.
Farragut, the Mississippi River was under the control of the North by the end of 1863. Large portions
of Louisiana and Mississippi were under a military
regime of the Union Army.

On December 8, 1863, the President offered pardon to "rebels" who would take the oath of allegiance to the Constitution and to the Union. By terms of that proclamation whenever a loyal nucleus, equal to one-tenth of the votes cast at the Presidential election in 1860, should qualify by taking the oath and by establishing a state government with abolition of slavery, he promised he would recognize it. The proclamation was offered all the seceding states except Virginia.

General Nathaniel P. Banks (in charge of Louisiana) ordered that an election for state officers be held in an area that included about one-third of that state. The voters declared eligible were 11,411 white men who had taken the oath of allegiance. The election was held on February 22, 1864, and three Congressmen and a Governor were chosen. Later, another election was held at which members of a Constitutional Convention were designated. That convention met the following April at New Orleans and adopted a constitution abolishing slavery "forever." The Constitution gave the ballot to white men only; but it empowered the legislature to give the ballot (1) to Negroes who had served in the Union Army and (2) to Negroes who could read.

This latter provision was in accord with a confidential suggestion that the President had made to the new Governor of Louisiana in a letter dated March 13, 1864:

"Hon. Michael Hahn

66

"My dear Sir:

"I congratulate you on having fixed your name in history as the first free-state Governor of Louisiana. Now you are about to have a Convention which, among other things, will probably define the elective franchise, I barely suggest for your private consideration, whether some of the colored people may not be let in—as, for instance, the very intelligent, and especially those who have fought gallantly in our ranks. They would probably help, in some trying time to come, to keep the jewel of liberty within the family of freedom. But this is only a suggestion, not to the public, but to you alone."

Arkansas likewise set up a new government, adopting in March, 1864, a new Constitution that abolished slavery and gave voting rights to every "free white male citizen." Arkansas then held an election and sent a delegation to Washington, D.C., which asked to be seated in Congress. The President had recognized the new government of Arkansas and the question was whether Congress would also do so. Under the Constitution it is for Congress to determine whether any delegation seeking to be seated lawfully represents a state or, if there be more than one, which will be admitted.

The Senate on June 29, 1864, voted 27 to 6 (with 16 absent) not to seat the Senators from Arkansas. Those in favor of the White House policy took the position stated by Senator Lane of Kansas: "It is enough that we are fighting people for seceding, without fighting with them for trying to get back into the Union."

Those against the White House policy thought that the election was not sufficiently representative. But overshadowing all issues was the clash over the kind of reconstruction program which should be adopted for the seceding states. Should it be one of leniency or one of severity?

The issue became sharper when Louisiana's case was presented to Congress in February, 1865.

The failure of Louisiana to grant the Negro voting rights aroused many Northerners. The Abolitionists and others maintained that the Negroes should have full rights of citizenship. One leading Abolitionist, however, shared the President's point of view. William Lloyd Garrison said, "Ever since the government was organized, the right of suffrage has been determined by each State in the Union for itself, so that there is no uniformity in regard to it. In some free States, colored citizens are allowed to vote; in others they are not. It is always a State, never a National matter."

Garrison was right on the facts and on the law. It was not until the Fifteenth Amendment, which became effective in 1868, that states were deprived of power to withhold the franchise from a Negro because of his race. In the 1860's, as the President knew, Negroes could not vote even in Illinois. For its constitution at that time gave the franchise only to "every white male citizen about the age of twenty-one years." Negroes in the 1860's could not vote in many other northern states. Not until 1870 were Negroes given that right in Illinois.

"When was it ever known that liberation from bondage was accompanied by a recognition of political equality?" Garrison asked. He added, "Coercion would gain nothing . . . universal suffrage will be hard to win and to hold without general preparation of feeling and sentiment. . . . I ask only charitable judgment of President Lincoln respecting this matter, whether in Louisiana or any other State."

Opposition to the recognition of the new government in Louisiana mounted. The President stood firm, thinking that "with such a nucleus around which to build, we could get the State into position again sooner than otherwise." He aimed first and always at putting back together all the pieces that made up the United States of America and making it possible for the nation to speak once more in one voice.

Trumbull spoke for him. He said that although the new Louisiana government controlled only one-third of the state's territory, the new Constitution was adopted by a representative group. "About two-thirds of the population of Louisiana and about two-thirds of the number of delegates of the whole State had been represented, and about two-thirds of the members of the Senate and of the House of Representatives, if the whole State had been represented, have taken part in this new government," Trumbull told the Senate. That is to say, "a majority of all the people of Louisiana" had expressed their preference for the new state government.

The majority of Congressmen and Senators were not impressed. Some were against it because they said the new government of Louisiana did not represent the people but only "the bayonets of General Banks and the will of the President."

Some said that since Negroes had not voted in the Louisiana election, the new state government was not properly formed. "If the loyal men, white and black, recognize it, then it will be Republican in form. Unless that is done, it will not be."

The answer was that the slavery issue, over which the war started, had been resolved in Louisiana in favor of freedom. The loyal men who lived there had abolished slavery and were now seeking admission to Congress. "They will never ask Congress to recognize any but an anti-slavery government." Moreover, to give Negroes the vote at once would create problems, they said. How could Northerners insist on Negroes voting in the South when they did not always have that right up North? One Senator stated:

"Maryland, by the constitution which she has just adopted, emancipates all her slaves, and without compensation; but she does not admit them to vote. They are excluded; and what would be the result if they were not excluded? There were seventy or eighty thousand free negroes in the State when the Constitution was adopted, and over seventy thousand slaves; altogether one hundred and forty or one hundred and fifty thousand Africans; about one-third of the whole population of the State. To suffer them to vote would be to control absolutely the intelligence of the State; to place us in the hands of an ignorant population; ignorant not because, perhaps, of any natural defect; ignorant not because of any fault of their own; ignorant because of the unhappy condition in which they have been placed. But that gives them no right to vote; because it would subject the State itself to very serious embarrassment, and perhaps to destruction."

Others pleaded that continuation of military rule in the seceding states was an evil policy, for if military rule continued "anarchy will reign supreme for many years hence, and outlaws and guerrillas, rejoicing in the anarchy and inefficiency of military rule, will mock your vain efforts to reestablish national authority. To secure national supremacy you must have the aid of State authority. For legitimate State authority you must rely upon the loyal voters."

The dominant view was the other way—that the federal government had the right to hold the seceding states "in the iron grip of war" and "as the conqueror, to rule and govern the state as conquered country, subject for a time at least to their sole will."

Hate and intolerance denounced the White

House-sponsored government of Louisiana: "The pretended State government in Louisiana is utterly indefensible whether you look at its origin or its character. . . . It is a mere seven-months' abortion, begotten by the bayonet in criminal conjunction with the spirit of caste, and born before its time, rickety, unformed, unfinished—whose continued existence will be a burden, a reproach, and a wrong. That is the whole case."

Because of that attitude, the House failed to approve the new Louisiana government by a vote of 80 to 65, with 37 members not voting. The Senate voted 34 to 12 to postpone a vote "to tomorrow"— a day that never came.

The dominant influences in the North wanted vengeance. The "rebel" leaders should be hanged. They left no room for compassion.

"If we shall suppose that American slavery is one of these offenses which, in the providence of God, must needs come, but which, having continued through his appointed time, he now wills to remove, and that he gives to both North and South this terrible war, as the woe due to those by whom the offense came, shall we discern therein any departure from those divine attributes which the believers in a Living God always ascribe to him?

"Fondly do we hope, fervently do we pray, that this mighty scourge of war may speedily pass away. Yet, if God wills that it continue until all the wealth piled by the bondsman's two hundred and fifty years of unrequited toil shall be sunk, and until every drop of blood drawn with the lash shall be paid by another drawn with the sword, as was said three thousand years ago, so still it must be said, 'The judgments of the Lord, are true and righteous altogether.' "

# SEVEN

GENERAL SHERMAN LATE IN 1864 MADE HIS FA-mous march across Georgia. In February, 1865, Sherman moved north into South Carolina. By the date of the Second Inaugural, Charleston and Columbia had fallen and Sherman was pushing into North Carolina. By the first part of April, 1865, Grant and Sheridan were pressing Lee at Petersburg and at Richmond. Petersburg was soon abandoned; then Richmond surrendered; and Lee bowed to Grant at Appomattox.

Lincoln proposed to treat the seceding states generously, not vindictively. Now that Lee had surrendered, he objected to imposing the will of the North on the South by military force. That also was the policy of McClellan, who had run against him in the 1864 election. One who had followed closely the campaign speeches in that election would have predicted that the South, once defeated, would be treated with lenience. Events, however, took a curious turn. A faction among the Republicans known as the Radicals had been very critical of the President, saying that he did not treat the South harshly

enough. That group—which was small at the time
of the 1864 election—eventually took command, and
before the end of 1865 fashioned a policy of vengeance.

When Lee surrendered, the South was in ruins.
Warehouses had been burned; lone chimneys
marked the sites of factories; bridges were down;
railroads were not operating. Food was short and
beggars filled the streets. Farms had no horses, cows,
pigs, or chickens. Now that the currency issued by
the Confederacy was worthless, wealthy men became
paupers. Many soldiers of the Confederacy had been
killed in the war. Homes and villages once calm and
peaceful were now places of desolation.

Federal troops occupied the principal cities, some
of these troops being Negroes—former slaves now
ruling their old masters. The continued presence of
troops annoyed the South, which—vanquished in
battle, stricken with poverty and desolation, and rid
of slavery—wanted to return peacefully to the Union. When Lee surrendered to Grant, Lee said that
"if the United States authorities desired it, the entire South could be restored to peace and harmony
in thirty days." Lee's invitation was not accepted.
Even though slavery was abolished, when the southern states asked to be readmitted to the Union, they
were turned down. Why?

If Lincoln had lived, that probably would not
have happened. For, though he too had suffered re-
verses in Congress, his political resourcefulness was

great. He was assassinated on Good Friday, April 14, 1865, while he sat in a box at the Ford Theatre watching a play. The assassin, John Wilkes Booth, crept up behind him, and, at a distance of five feet, pulled the trigger of a vest-pocket pistol that sent a bullet into his brain. He never regained consciousness and died the next day.

Andrew Johnson, the Vice-President, succeeded to the Presidency and in the main Johnson pursued his predecessor's policy. But the Congress, under the growing power of the Radical Republicans, was opposed to leniency and conciliation. Johnson on one side and the Radical Republicans on the other became engaged in a bitter struggle. The issue was, how should the defeated South be treated? The Radical Republicans, extreme in their vindictiveness, tried to remove Johnson through the procedure of impeachment. The House brought the charges against Johnson and the Senate sat as a court to determine whether Johnson was guilty or not guilty. The Radicals failed by one vote to get Johnson impeached; and he continued as President until the end of his term.

Grant was elected President in 1868 and again in 1872, remaining in office until the election of Rutherford B. Hayes in 1876. In the intervening twelve years—from Lincoln's death to 1877—the Radical Republicans stayed in control of Congress and inflicted a cruel regime on the South. The plan of reconstruction which the martyred President had in

mind was not wholly known. But its main outlines
were clear from what he said on April 11, 1865, just
three days before he was assassinated:

"Some twelve thousand voters in the heretofore
slave-state of Louisiana have sworn allegiance to the
Union, assumed to be the rightful political power of
the State, held elections, organized a State government, adopted a free-state constitution, giving the
benefit of public schools equally to black and white,
and empowering the Legislature to confer the elective franchise upon the colored man. Their Legislature has already voted to ratify the constitutional
amendment recently passed by Congress, abolishing
slavery throughout the nation. These twelve thousand persons are thus fully committed to the Union,
and to perpetual freedom in the state—committed to
the very things, and nearly all the things the nation
wants—and they ask the nation's recognition, and its
assistance to make good their committal.

"Now, if we reject, and spurn them, we do our
utmost to disorganize and disperse them. We in effect
say to the white men 'You are worthless, or worse—
we will neither help you, nor be helped by you.' To
the blacks we say 'This cup of liberty which these,
your old masters, hold to your lips, we will dash from
you, and leave you to the chances of gathering the
spilled and scattered contents in some vague and un-
defined when, where, and how.'

"If this course, discouraging and paralyzing both
white and black, has any tendency to bring Louisiana

into proper practical relations with the Union, I have, so far, been unable to perceive it.

"If, on the contrary, we recognize, and sustain the new government of Louisiana, the converse of all this is made true. We encourage the hearts, and nerve the arms of the twelve thousand to adhere to their work, and argue for it, and proselyte for it, and fight for it, and feed it, and grow it, and ripen it to a complete success.

"The colored man too, in seeing all united for him, is inspired with vigilance, and energy, and daring, to the same end. Grant that he desires the elective franchise, will he not attain it sooner by saving the already advanced steps toward it, than by running backward over them? Concede that the new government of Louisiana is only to what it should be as the egg is to the fowl, we shall sooner have the fowl by hatching the egg than by smashing it. . . ."

He was willing to forgive the "rebels," to give them back all their property, except the slaves. He was willing to recognize any state government in the South that abolished slavery provided that the new regime was established by voters who took the loyalty oath and who equaled one-tenth of the votes cast in that state in the 1860 Presidential election.

Johnson pursued that course. He did not seek revenge for past acts; he tried to heal the wounds of war.

The victors in the Civil War—unlike Fidel Castro of Cuba—did not try the leaders of the defeated group nor execute them. Some were arrested; Jefferson Davis was indeed held in prison for about two years. But in the end all prosecutions were dropped and every southern leader was pardoned.

Lincoln hoped Jefferson Davis would escape when the war was ended. He had a story he told when asked what he would do if he captured Davis:

"When I was a boy in Indiana, I went to a neighbor's house one morning and found a boy of my own size holding a coon by a string. I asked him what he had and what he was doing. He says, 'It's a coon. Dad cotched six last night, and killed all but this poor little cuss. Dad told me to hold him until he came back, and I'm afraid he's going to kill this one too; and oh, Abe, I do wish he would get away!' 'Well, why don't you let him loose?' 'That wouldn't be right; and if I let him go, Dad would give me hell. But if he would get away himself, it would be all right.'

"Now," he said, "if Jeff Davis and those other fellows will only get away, it will be all right. But if we should catch them, and I should let them go, 'Dad would give me hell.' "

The "Dad" that he referred to was, of course, the people of the North, who had lost thousands of sons and husbands in battle. But their passions soon cooled and in the end they, like the Great Emancipator, showed compassion.

Johnson wanted to restore the seceding states to the Union as quickly as possible—through normal democratic processes, not through military force. By December, 1865, all the seceding states, except Texas, had met his requirements for readmission. They had elected Senators and Congressmen and sent them to Washington, D.C., to be seated.

This plan for reconciliation was rejected by Congress when it met in December, 1865. The Radical Republicans, led by Thaddeus Stevens of Pennsylvania, called the "rebels" of the South "traitors." They must be "punished," Stevens said. Their property must be taken to pay "the cost of the war." The lands of the rebels must be distributed among the ex-slaves—forty acres to each family head. Negroes must be given the right to vote—"if it be punishment to traitors, they deserve it."

Johnson, like his predecessor, was not against Negro suffrage; both realized, however, that people just coming out of slavery and almost entirely illiterate might not be qualified as yet to vote. Both were willing to see Negro suffrage gradually adopted. But the Radical Republicans, bent on vengeance, shared none of that tolerance.

The seceding states that asked to be readmitted to the Union in 1865 had passed new laws defining the civil rights of the Negroes. These laws were denounced by the Radical Republicans as Black Codes designed to reintroduce slavery.

These Black Codes gave Negroes some rights—the right to sue and be sued, the right to acquire and dispose of property and to inherit it, the right to be witnesses in courts. But the Black Codes were in the main discriminatory. Negroes needed licenses showing where they lived and worked. If they broke a contract to work, they forfeited all their wages. A Negro who quit a job could be retaken by the police, who got a fee for this service plus ten cents a mile from the place of arrest to the place of delivery, these charges to be paid by the employer and withheld from the Negro's wages. Young Negroes could be apprenticed to white families and they too were under strict surveillance. It was made a crime for a Negro or mulatto to marry a white person. Under some codes an unemployed Negro was a vagrant; and a vagrant could be fined and sentenced to work out his fine on a white man's private plantation. These codes had other features that discriminated against Negroes. Negroes were segregated in all public facilities. Negroes were sometimes restricted as to the land they could own. They could not bear arms. Only white people could vote.

The Radicals imposed their own ideas on the South. While Tennessee was readmitted to the Union in July, 1866, the other seceding states went through agonizing years before they were readmitted.

The oppressive laws passed by Congress were numerous. The most oppressive ones divided the ten southern states still not readmitted into the Union into five military districts and put federal army officers in charge of these districts. These army officers were made superior to the state governments.

They could make arrests; they could establish military courts to try anyone for most crimes; they could make almost anything a crime, even the writing of a newspaper editorial that was critical of the army; the army could, in other words, take over and exercise the powers of the state governments.

Congress also created a federal agency known as the Freedmen's Bureau to operate in the South. This bureau not only cared for ex-slaves; it was empowered to displace state courts and to transfer cases from those courts to military tribunals. The idea was that only the Army could be trusted to enforce the civil rights of Negroes. But the creation of military courts to hear civil cases in times of peace violated many constitutional guarantees, including the right to trial by jury. That was one reason Johnson vetoed the bill. But Congress passed it over his veto.

The Freedmen's Bureau rendered good service to Negroes by helping them find their way as free men. But the bureau became a hated thing in the South. The special courts it created to serve the needs of Negroes aroused resentment. Some of its officials were corrupt. It became, moreover, a political agency playing local politics to make sure that the Radical Republicans controlled the vital areas in the South.

Under the reconstruction laws the military governors were to register voters, hold elections, and choose delegates for conventions to adopt not only the Fourteenth Amendment but also the new state constitutions which would meet the Radical Republicans' demands. While Negroes were to be enrolled as voters, any white person who had served in the government of the Confederacy was permanently to be barred from voting.

Thousands of Northerners went south to serve as federal officials, to control southern political machines, to make money, and to run the southern governments for the Radical Republicans. They were called "carpetbaggers"—a word descriptive of the type of suitcases or valises which travelers at that time carried with them. They worked with the "scalawags"—whites in the South who conspired with the "carpetbaggers" either to get into office or to make money.

The voters registered by the Army were largely Negroes, carpetbaggers, and scalawags. Elections became corrupt. Negroes were marched from precinct to precinct, voting many times.

The Radical Republicans insisted that the new state constitutions must be adopted by a majority of all registered voters. The whites in Alabama, therefore, decided to *register* but not to *vote*. They stayed away from the polls. As a result, only 70,000 out of 167,000 registered voters approved the new constitutions, which was not a majority. Accordingly, the Radical Republicans passed a new law which provided that a majority of all votes cast, no matter how small, would be sufficient to adopt a state constitution. The new law also provided that a person was qualified to vote if he had resided in the election district for ten days prior to the election. The purpose was to put the Negroes and the carpetbaggers in control, and that in fact happened.

In June, 1868, Arkansas, Florida, Louisiana, North Carolina, and South Carolina were admitted to the Union. The next month Alabama was admitted. Georgia, Mississippi, Virginia, and Texas, however, were not admitted until 1870, five years after the end of the war.

Congress proposed to all the states the Fourteenth Amendment. This Amendment (drawn primarily to protect Negroes though not restricted to them) was finally ratified in 1868. It did the following:

First, it made everyone born in the United States a citizen.

Second, it provided that a state should not "deprive any person of life, liberty, or property, without due process of law." (This clause has had far-reaching effects, for example, in forbidding the states to deny a person basic liberties, such as freedom of speech and press, freedom of religion and freedom from torture at the hands of the police.)

Third, it provided that a state should not deprive a person of "equal protection of the laws." (This clause, too, has had important consequences. The idea of "equal protection" was eventually construed by the courts to mean that segregation of Negroes in public facilities was not constitutional.)

Congress also proposed the adoption of the Fifteenth Amendment, which was ratified in 1870. The

Fifteenth Amendment provides that "The right of citizens of the United States to vote shall not be denied or abridged by the United States or by any State on account of race, color, or previous condition of servitude."

Georgia, Mississippi, Virginia, and Texas were required to approve this Amendment, as well as the Fourteenth Amendment, prior to their admission into the Union.

Yet the Union Army remained in control of the southern states even after they had been admitted into the Union. Opportunists made fortunes. It was common for officials to make more from bribery than from salaries. In South Carolina, $835,000 was appropriated for printing in one period of fifteen months, while over the previous seventy-eight *years* only $609,000 had been spent in printing. Men bribed legislators to get state bond issues approved. The proceeds of the bond sales were stolen or misappropriated. The indebtedness of the southern states increased by staggering amounts. Tax rates in Mississippi in 1874 increased fourteen times over what they had been in 1869. In North Carolina twenty-four million dollars of bonds were issued by the Radical Republican machine to their friends.

Militias were formed by these state governments, acting as puppets for the Radical Republicans. Some were made up of whites; some, of Negroes. They raided and plundered farms, stealing property and running off stock. White militiamen fought Negro militiamen; race riots occurred. But the real purpose behind the militias was graft. The militias were merely the cloak whereby huge sums were taken out of the public treasury for the benefit of the henchmen of the Radical Republicans.

The corrupt and exploitative practices of the carpetbaggers and the scalawags created bitter resentment among the southern people. It was then that the Ku Klux Klan was formed. The Klan was made up of white-robed and hooded men who rode at night to frighten the Negroes away from the polls and to threaten carpetbaggers and scalawags.

But the Klan played only a minor role in eliminating the carpetbaggers and the scalawags and in driving the Radical Republicans from office. The graft and corruption were so vast and became so scandalous that public opinion finally forced the Radical Republicans out.

Georgia, North Carolina, Tennessee, and Virginia were the first to get rid of them. Alabama, Arkansas, and Texas were next. But even as late as 1876— eleven years after the Second Inaugural—the Radical Republicans still ruled Florida, Louisiana, and South Carolina. In these three states the Army remained in occupation. The votes of those states were necessary if the Republicans were to win the 1876 elections. Rutherford B. Hayes was the Republican candidate; Samuel J. Tilden, the Democratic candidate. One hundred and eighty-five electoral votes were necessary to win. When the votes were totaled,

Tilden had 184 and Hayes had 166 without counting Florida, Louisiana, and South Carolina. These
states had 19 votes. Their 19, plus the 166, gave
Hayes a total of 185, making him President by one
vote. Those three states went into the Republican
column only because the Radical Republicans supported by the Army were in control of the election
machinery. Had the election been fair, Tilden would
have won. But frauds were committed in making
the election returns in those three states. We now
know that the Radical Republicans destroyed enough
Democratic votes to carry those states. The scandals
shocked the country.

Hayes responded quickly. He withdrew the Army
from those three states and the oppressive period of
reconstruction at last came to an end—twelve years
after the Second Inaugural had announced "with
malice toward none" as the national policy.

Lincoln would have opposed any regime that
exalted one race over the other. He knew that the
Negroes, long in slavery, uneducated, and with never
a chance to participate as citizens in the affairs of
their communities, would not be ready for those tasks
overnight. But he planned that all men—no matter
their race or nationality—would be equal before the
law and in time have equal rights of citizenship with
all other men.

His denunciation of slavery was good for all nations and for all times. His method for getting rid of
it was not force and violence such as John Brown

used when he captured Harpers Ferry. He thought John Brown showed "great courage, rare unselfishness." But no man, "North or South," he said, "can approve of violence or crime." His means of eradicating evil, of remedying a wrong, was political action: "We have a means provided for the expression of our belief in regard to slavery—it is through the ballot box—the peaceful method provided by the Constitution."

His plea for political equality was in the same vein; there, too, he called for political action, not violence. His plea for equality had the same universal appeal as his denunciation of slavery. He did not wage class warfare; he did not exploit differences between classes. His creed was the very antithesis of Communism, whose principles were first announced in 1848. Rich and poor, black and white, Jew and Christian, workingman and banker—each of these stood equally before the law and was entitled to equal justice. "That some should be rich shows that others may become rich, and hence is just encouragement to industry and enterprise. Let not him who is houseless pull down the house of another, but let him work, diligently and build one for himself, thus by example assuring that his own shall be safe from violence when built."

On February 22, 1861, just before the First Inauguration, he said that the Declaration of Independence gave "liberty not alone to the people of this country but hope to the world for all future time."

And he added, "It was that which gave promise that in due time the weights should be lifted from the shoulders of all men, and that *all* should have an equal chance."

That idea carries "charity" to every benighted people. Christ spoke of faith, hope, and charity—"but the greatest of these is charity." The Second Inaugural gives the idea a distinctive American flavor. The phrase becomes identified with the racial problem. It asks for tolerance of man toward his fellow man whatever his race, his creed, his color. It pleads for tolerance of a diversity of views. Truth is elusive; no one has a patent on it; the market place of ideas should be free and open.

"With malice toward none; with charity for all; with firmness in the right, as God gives us to see the right, let us strive on to finish the work we are in; to bind up the nation's wounds; to care for him who shall have borne the battle and for his widow, and his orphan—to do all which may achieve and cherish a just and lasting peace among ourselves, and with all nations."

# EIGHT

L INCOLN OFTEN SPOKE OF THE DECLARATION OF IN-
dependence and its statement that "all men
are created equal." To him those words were "the
electric cord . . . that links the hearts of patriotic
and liberty-loving men together, that will link those
patriotic hearts as long as the love of freedom exists
in the minds of men throughout the world."

Early in his public life he had pointed out that
slavery was not consistent with the Declaration of
Independence. ". . . We began by declaring that all
men are created equal; but now from that beginning
we have run down to the other declaration, that
*some* men to enslave *others* is a 'sacred right of self-
government.' . . . If it had been said in Old Independence Hall, seventy-eight years ago, the very
door-keeper would have throttled the man, and thrust
him into the street."

In the debates of the 1850's some declared that,
when the Declaration of Independence stated that
all men are created equal, it meant only that "British
subjects on this continent" were "equal to British
subjects born and residing in Great Britain." Lin-

coln's answer was that in that view "the French, Germans, and other white people of the world are all gone to pot" along with the blacks, browns, and yellows. The opposition then changed its position and maintained that the equality clause of the Declaration of Independence meant "white men, men of European birth and European descent, and had no reference either to the Negro, the savage Indians, the Fiji, the Malay, or any other inferior and degraded race."

The man who maintained that all men, irrespective of race, creed, or color, were equal before the law called the Declaration of Independence the "immortal emblem of Humanity" because it gave "to the whole great family of man" the right to life, liberty, and the pursuit of happiness. He maintained that it "applies to the slave as well as to ourselves, that the class of arguments put forward to batter down that idea, are also calculated to break down the very idea of a free government, even for white men, and to undermine the very foundations of a free society."

He said, "The Saviour, I suppose, did not expect that any human creature could be perfect as the Father in Heaven; but He said, 'As your Father in Heaven is perfect, be ye also perfect.' He set that up as a standard, and he who did most towards reaching that standard, attained the highest degree of moral perfection. So I say in relation to the principle that all men are created equal, let it be as nearly reached

as we can. If we cannot give freedom to every creature, let us do nothing that will impose slavery upon
any other creature."

In Lincoln's day the Know-Nothings were opposed to Negroes, foreigners, and Catholics. As early
as 1855, he denounced the Know-Nothings. "As a
nation," he wrote, "we began by declaring that *'all
men are created equal.'* We now practically read it
'all men are created equal, *except negroes.'* When
the Know-Nothings get control, it will read 'all men
are created equal, except negroes, *and foreigners, and
Catholics.'* When it comes to this I should prefer emi-
grating to some country where they make no pretense of loving liberty—to Russia, for instance, where
despotism can be taken pure, and without the base
alloy of hypocrisy."

The Declaration of Independence would give men
courage in distant days "to renew the battle which
their fathers began—so that truth and justice and
mercy and all the humane and Christian virtues
might not be extinguished from the land, so that
no man would hereafter dare to limit and circum-
scribe the great principles on which the temple of
justice was being built." Early in his life Lincoln
spoke of the force and power of the Declaration of
Independence:

"Of our political revolution of '76, we all are justly
proud. It has given us a degree of political freedom,
far exceeding that of any other of the nations of the
earth. In it the world has found a solution of that

long mooted problem, as to the capability of man to govern himself. In it was the germ which has vegetated, and still is to grow and expand into the universal liberty of mankind."

That germ has yet to take root in most areas and had not done so even in the North during the Civil War. Negroes in the Union Army suffered discrimination. Colored troops were segregated from white troops, yet made to serve under white officers. The Negro soldiers did not receive the same pay as white soldiers, whites receiving $13 a month plus allowances for clothing and the Negroes $7 a month. In 1862, the Negroes' salary was raised to $10 a month. Finally, in 1864, Congress provided that all Negroes who were free before April 19, 1861—the date the first call for troops was made—were to receive the same pay as white soldiers. On March 3, 1865, all Negroes who had been taken into the Army on assurance by the President or Secretary of War that they would get equal pay were granted it. The Civil War ended, however, without all Negroes in military service receiving the same pay as the whites rendering the same service.

That inequality in treatment cast a long shadow across the pages of American history. The Negro, though freed, suffered discrimination even when he was a soldier or sailor. Not until the 1940's were steps taken to end the practice of segregating Negroes in the Armed Services. Not until 1954 was segregation in the Armed Services completely and finally uprooted—a provision that has not, however, been extended to the National Guard.

The end of that regime of segregation has had continuous, as well as immediate benefits, as summarized by the 1961 United States Commission on Civil Rights Report on Employment:

"The Armed Forces of the United States offer work opportunities second in quantity only to the civilian establishment of the Federal Government. In breadth of training opportunities they are second to none, offering training in almost every type of skill and learning either through their own facilities or through reimbursement to private institutions. To the Negro, who is often discriminatorily denied such opportunities as a civilian, enlistment in the Armed Forces is particularly attractive. Thus many Negroes have elected to become military career men. Others have acquired skills through military training which have enabled them to qualify for civilian jobs—particularly those requiring technical skills—which would not otherwise have been open to them."

After the Civil War, the northern states opened inns, theaters, and other public facilities to all races. By 1870, Illinois had extended the franchise to Negroes. But though most of the states made racial discrimination unlawful, discrimination continued in various forms throughout the nation—from the 1860's to the 1960's.

After the Civil War some southern states provided that there should be no segregation in public schools.

Those laws, however, were soon repealed; and segregation became the way of life, fortified by custom and by law. Public facilities—such as parks, railroad cars, restaurants, theaters, schools, waiting rooms, and toilets—were racially segregated by state laws. The validity of those laws was squarely presented to the Court over thirty years after the Civil War was ended. At that time the Court was composed of Chief Justice Fuller of Illinois, Field of California, Gray of Massachusetts, Brewer of Kansas, Brown of Michigan, Shiras of Pennsylvania, White of Louisiana, Peckham of New York, and Harlan of Kentucky. Of the nine, only White was from the South. Harlan, from the Border State of Kentucky, was once a slaveowner. All of the judges from the North plus White, the sole Southerner, joined in *Plessy* v. *Ferguson,* 163 U.S. 537, to decide on May 18, 1896, that a state's segregation of the races in passenger trains was not a denial of "equal protection of the laws" within the meaning of the Fourteenth Amendment. The opinion was written by Brown, who commented for the Court on the meaning of that clause:

"The object of the amendment was undoubtedly to enforce the absolute equality of the two races before the law, but in the nature of things it could not have been intended to abolish distinctions based upon color, or to enforce social, as distinguished from political equality, or a commingling of the two races upon terms unsatisfactory to either. Laws permitting, and even requiring, their separation in places where they are liable to be brought into contact do not necessarily imply the inferiority of either race to the other, and have been generally, if not universally, recognized as within the competency of the state legislatures in the exercise of their police power. The most common instance of this is connected with the establishment of separate schools for white and colored children, which has been held to be a valid exercise of the legislative power even by courts of States where the political rights of the colored race have been longest and most earnestly enforced." 163 U.S. at 544.

It was argued that if a state legislature could segregate the races in railroad coaches, it could enact laws "requiring colored people to walk upon one side of the street, and white people upon the other, or requiring white men's houses to be painted white, and colored men's black, or their vehicles or business signs to be of different colors, upon the theory that one side of the street is as good as the other, or that a house or vehicle of one color is as good as one of another color." *Id.* at 549, 550. The Court answered by saying that every exercise of the police power of a State must be "reasonable" and enacted "for the promotion of the public good and not for the annoyance or oppression of a particular class." Thus it rejected *apartheid* carried to its ultimate end as in South Africa. It upheld segregation of the races in public facilities provided the "separate" facilities granted the Negroes were "equal" to those used by the whites. (A

phrase coined by the dissenter. See *Id.* at 552.) A
state, the Court ruled, could put its weight behind
the racial bias or prejudice of the dominant group in
the community, making that bias or prejudice the
state's policy.

The first Mr. Justice Harlan was the sole dissenter. He stated what was to become sixty years later
the prevailing construction of the Equal Protection
Clause of the Fourteenth Amendment:

". . . in view of the Constitution, in the eye of
the law, there is in this country no superior, dominant, ruling class of citizens. There is no caste here.
Our Constitution is color-blind, and neither knows
nor tolerates classes among citizens. In respect of civil
rights, all citizens are equal before the law. The humblest is the peer of the most powerful. The law regards man as man, and takes no account of his surroundings or of his color when his civil rights as
guaranteed by the supreme law of the land are involved." *Plessy* v. *Ferguson* at 559.

He added:

"The destinies of the two races, in this country, are
indissolubly linked together, and the interests of
both require that the common government of all
shall not permit the seeds of race hate to be planted
under the sanction of law. What can more certainly
arouse race hate, what more certainly create and
perpetuate a feeling of distrust between these races,
than state enactments, which, in fact, proceed on the
ground that colored citizens are so inferior and de-

graded that they cannot be allowed to sit in public coaches occupied by white citizens?" *Id.* at 560.

Negroes have also been discriminated against at the polls. By the 1960's the percentage of Negroes registered as voters was only about 4 percent of all voting-age Negroes in Mississippi and 40 percent in Florida, with an overall average of 28 percent as compared with an overall average of 56 percent for southern whites.

Various devices were used to keep the Negro from voting. Racial gerrymandering (which the courts in time struck down) reduced the proportionate weight of Negro votes or eliminated them entirely from municipal affairs. There were other deterrents. Some states, including northern ones, have used poll taxes to raise money for the support of the government. These taxes are laid upon persons without regard to their occupations or property and may amount to one dollar a year or more. States that collected poll taxes customarily required the poll tax to be paid before a person could vote; and that requirement was sustained, since in our federal system the qualifications of voters are determined by the states, save as the Constitution restrains them. While the tax for each year might not be great, arrears had to be paid; and the total amount due might be $15, $20, $25, or more. The pinch of the poll tax was on the poor; and since Negroes were usually poor, the poll tax discouraged them from voting. Congress finally adopted a resolution in 1962 proposing a Constitutional Amendment that would abolish the poll tax as a condition to voting in a Presidential election or in an election for Senator or Representative in Congress.

Literacy is not synonymous with intelligence. Even illiterate, unsophisticated people can vote intelligently. India, under Nehru, is an example. In spite of an overall illiteracy rate of 78 percent, Indians have voted with discernment in municipal, state, and national elections. Seldom have they been seduced by the wiles of the Communist party; they have kept India solidly in the democratic ranks.

Under our constitutional system qualifications of voters have been entrusted to the states. There are exceptions—the Fifteenth Amendment denies a state the power to withhold voting rights on account of race, color, or previous condition of servitude, and the Nineteenth bars denial of voting rights on account of sex. If a literacy test is not used as a cloak to bar a person from voting because of race or sex, it is constitutional. Such legislation may not be wise; but the power to prescribe literacy requirements has been sustained.

It has at times been used only as a cloak for violating the Fifteenth Amendment.

In some areas the Citizens Councils—organized to prevent assertion by Negroes of their rights—comb through registration records looking for Negro registrations that might be challenged on the grounds of illiteracy. A Negro registrant is easy to detect, since the color of the registrant is often disclosed on the card. Once these files are combed, many minor errors —both on the parts of whites and blacks—can be found. The Negro who makes a mistake is stricken from the rolls while a white voter is not. One Negro woman was removed because her age was incorrectly computed by one day if the date on which the registration card was executed was counted. A Negro man was removed because he misspelled the county of his birth. Yet those who challenged him themselves spelled the word "misspelled" incorrectly. A Negro who in describing his color used the letter "C" rather than the word Colored was stricken, though a white person who used the letter "W" was not. All Negro registrants in some wards were challenged, while none of the whites were; over-all 100 or 150 Negro registrants were examined while only two or three white ones were. Moreover, more than 60 percent of the white registrations had deficiencies on their cards like those for which Negroes were challenged. Yet white voters went unchallenged while Negroes were stricken.

Laws were passed in some states which qualified as a voter anyone whose ancestor was eligible to vote on January 1, 1866. All whites were therefore qualified, provided their grandfathers were not aliens, criminals, and the like. A twentieth-century Negro's grandfather, however, had probably been a slave. Even though "free" in 1866 he had not been allowed to vote. So his grandson or granddaughter, unlike the white voter, was required to take a literacy test. These laws were held unconstitutional.

In some states the primary election (where candidates are chosen to run in the general election) is a vital election, as the person who wins the Democratic primary is practically certain of winning in the general election. Some states enacted laws that only white people could vote in their primaries. Those laws were finally held unconstitutional.

Yet, in spite of discrimination, Negro votes at times have been a decisive factor in close elections. They caused Louisiana and Tennessee to go Republican in 1956, and provided a margin of victory in a number of counties in other states. Negro votes gave Kennedy his 9,561-vote victory over Nixon in North Carolina in 1960. Negroes were elected to public office in Georgia, South Carolina, North Carolina, Tennessee, Texas, and Virginia in the 1950's and 1960's. These Negro office holders constitute a very small minority; yet they are scattered throughout many local units, including school boards and planning commissions. Though the white voters in the South outnumber the Negro voter by over 12 to 1, the whites have promised Negroes equality in employment and other civil rights. For the Negro vote, once purchased by politicians, has become more and more conscious of its power, and candidates are catering more and more to Negro interests.

Poor educational facilities for the Negro have proved to be his greatest deterrent, as Booker T.

Washington forecast in *Up from Slavery*.

The lack of good educational facilities is reflected in statistics showing that service and other nonskilled, nonfarm occupations employ about 47 percent of Negro workers and 14 percent of white workers. Only 12 percent of Negro workers are in professional, managerial, and white collar occupations, compared to about 42 percent of white workers. The median family income for Negroes is about 30 percent below the median for the whites. The rate of unemployment for Negroes is double that for whites.

Through the years, discrimination as respects education has been notorious. Usually the Negro school has been inferior to the white school both in instruction and educational standards. Negroes sued in the courts claiming that the segregated schools, which they were required to attend, were not equal to the white schools. Over and again the courts ruled that the facilities were not equal and that therefore the Negroes should be admitted to the white schools. Some states tried to solve the problem by giving Negroes scholarships to attend out-of-state schools. The courts ruled that this was a subterfuge and not allowable. Some white schools, after admitting a Negro under compulsion, required him to sit in a row apart from the whites or to use only a segregated part of the school library. The courts held that this device was not constitutional. Finally cases arose where it was contended that the schools of Negroes in fact were equal to those of the whites. And so the question was presented, were the old decisions (holding segregation constitutional if "separate but equal" facilities were made available to Negroes) still valid?

If state laws had required segregation in public schools of Jews and Gentiles, who would have been so bold as to maintain that those laws were constitutional? But the background of slavery had long plagued the Negro and put his case in a different frame of reference.

Finally, the Court in 1954 decided *Brown* v. *Board of Education of Topeka*, 347 U.S. 483, holding that the "separate but equal" doctrine was unconstitutional; that neither a state nor the federal government could require the races to be segregated in public schools; that the American Constitution was "color blind." Segregation, it was said, was not that "equal protection" of the law that the Fourteenth Amendment guarantees every person against hostile state action.

By coincidence the Court that decided the *Brown* case also had on it only one Southerner—Hugo L. Black—and one from Kentucky, Stanley Reed. While *Plessy* v. *Ferguson* was decided in favor of segregation eight to one, the *Brown* case was decided the other way in a unanimous opinion.

Some criticized the Court for overruling a sixty-year-old precedent. But the Court has never viewed constitutional decisions as permanent fixtures beyond the power of recall. It has frequently overruled cases construing the Constitution, since the oath a justice takes is to support the Constitution, not the gloss that some predecessor put on it. In 1938 the Court overruled an earlier constitutional decision having nothing to do with racial problems and which had been decided ninety-six years earlier. Between 1937 and 1949 the Court had in fact overruled thirty prior constitutional decisions. What the Court did in the *Brown* case was therefore in a great tradition. The practice of courts undoing their own wrongs is a healthy one. It heeds Shakespeare's warning in *The Merchant of Venice:*

> 'Twill be recorded for a precedent;
> And many an error by the same example
> Will rush into the state.

In spite of progress made in complying with the 1954 decision, there were at the end of 1961 over two thousand school districts in the South that had not even started to comply with it. There was also school segregation in the North, East, and West, resulting largely from neighborhood schools that served residential concentrations of Negroes. But the South is not alone in noncompliance. In Chicago segregation in the schools increased from 85 percent to 92 percent between 1958 and 1962. Some communities used gerrymandering to fix boundaries of school districts so as to produce segregated schools; and those projects, when challenged in the courts, were set aside.

Meanwhile, suits were brought by Negroes claiming they were denied sleeping accommodations on interstate railroads or were required to sit apart on interstate buses. In other suits Negroes complained that they had been denied the right to vacant seats in railroad dining cars, or denied access to public parks, public beaches, public golf courses. These cases, like those involving public schools, were decided in favor of the Negroes. Yet not until 1961 was segregation of races on interstate trains and buses and in interstate terminals banned by an all-inclusive regulation of the Interstate Commerce Commission.

Negroes have not been given equal opportunity, even in work. Prior to 1961 there was no Negro physician on the *regular* staff of any *private* New York City hospital, though a few extended courtesy privileges to Negro physicians. Up to 1941 most of the *public* hospitals in New York City did not allow Negroes on their in-staffs. Negroes were not allowed to eat in white restaurants in the nation's capital until 1953.

In 1945, New York and New Jersey passed comprehensive laws forbidding discrimination in employment on account of race, creed, color, or national origin. Some twenty states had adopted that kind of law by the 1960's. In 1961 President Kennedy issued a comprehensive executive order banning discrimination based on race, creed, color, or national origin both in federal employment and in employment by contractors or sub-contractors doing work for the federal government.

By the mid-1950's most unions had opened their membership to Negroes as well as whites. But, as we entered the 1960's, one of the largest unions barred them from membership.

Even when Negroes are not admitted to membership in a union, the union is often the bargaining agent for all employees—white and black. The union must therefore, the Courts say, act impartially and not discriminate against one race and in favor of the other.

The average annual income of a Negro family is not much more than 50 percent of the average annual income of the white family. When unemployment comes, Negroes are among the first to be affected. The unemployment figures for the early 1960's in some of the leading cities show that Negro unemployment comes close to national unemployment in the days of the Great Depression. With automation and other technological developments, more skilled labor may be required and by the same token the unskilled laborers will find it increasingly difficult to get jobs. Yet a Negro unskilled laborer has difficulty moving up the escalator into a skilled job.

Some forty national and international unions have civil rights committees to make sure that there is no discrimination in employment. Yet discrimination persists. A 1961 report showed that of the 3,500 apprentices in all trades in Newark, New Jersey, only two were Negroes. A 1961 Chicago study showed that, while 25 percent of that city's population was Negro, less than 1 percent of all apprentices in Chicago were Negroes. In Detroit only one Negro had ever participated in the automobile workers' apprentice program. In the North, while vocational training is open to all, few Negroes have become skilled mechanics for the reason that craft unions in practice would not admit them. Thus even in the North vocational training has largely been for the whites, the Negroes being trained for more menial tasks, such as shoe repairing, tailoring, and plastering. Even when a Negro was admitted to a craft union, he was assigned lower-paid work or no work at all. And even though he was a union member, when he moved from one section of the country to another, the union would often not recognize his union card.

As we entered the 1960's many communities still barred Negroes from jury duty; in others they were excluded from white restaurants, white parks, white movies—although decisions of the Court make clear that any segregation enforced as a matter of municipal policy is unconstitutional.

Segregation in housing is still the rule, not the exception. Many deeds to real estate located in residential areas long provided that the property would not be sold to Negroes, to Mexicans, to Jews. The courts by the 1950's had refused to enforce these restrictions. Yet in many areas real estate brokers still will not sell Negroes property in white residential areas; in some cities zoning boards have refused permits to build schools that were to be integrated.

The prejudices of property owners have been encouraged by real estate brokers, builders, and the financial community upon which mortgage financing depends. Those groups, with few exceptions, have maintained that only a "homogeneous" neighborhood assures economic soundness. Seventeen states and a number of cities have adopted laws and ordinances to eliminate racial discrimination in housing. But at the beginning of the 1960's the federal government, though heavily involved in financing housing and related projects, had done very little to remove racial discrimination in that area. In Chicago residential segregation increased from 92 percent to 93 percent between 1950 and 1960.

The cause of equality of the races which Lincoln espoused as an American ideal has not been wholly fulfilled either in the North or South or East or West. Abroad, Americans are often chided about it. After World War II, Mrs. Edith Sampson, a Negro lawyer from Chicago, visited India and was questioned by members of an audience: "Why do they lynch Negroes in America? Why are they not given a fair trial?" She shook her finger at the inquirer, saying, "I fight for the rights of the Negroes at home. But here in India let me say this: no minority race has made greater progress than the American Negro since the Civil War."

The Negro has indeed made greater progress in this nation than any racial minority in a like length of time in any other nation in any area of the world.

The classless society of the Second Inaugural exists in very few areas of the world. Equality among men is today more often than not dishonored on the other continents. The new Constitution of India abolishes legal distinctions based on caste, but caste prejudice, deeply rooted in custom, still continues. In some Asian countries—Indonesia, the Philippines, and Thailand—Chinese are barred from certain industries and from many trades. Overseas Chinese in Southeast Asia are sometimes not even allowed to vote, to own land, or to hold office.

In South Africa, Negroes are segregated, deprived of civil rights, and relegated to an inferior citizenship.

In Communist countries, class lines are strictly drawn. The preferred class is made up of party members. They get the extra ration coupons, the largest apartments, the automobiles. In southern Russia— which is made up of minority races—there is a segregated school system. In southern Russia, a Russian gets 130 percent of the salary which a member of a minority race receives for doing the same work. Friendship University in Moscow was organized in order to segregate Asian and African students from Russian students. In Russia the identification papers of a Jew are stamped "Jew"; and it is a crime to teach the Hebrew language.

Some Moslem nations relegate Hindus and Jews to second-class citizenship. Turkey, modern both in political organization and in technology, bears down fiercely on her Kurdish minority and even bars the use of the Kurdish language. In northern Iran the same despised minority, the Kurds, though nominally given equal protection of the laws, is in practice not admitted to public office. Christians in Pakistan, though not persecuted, have a keen sense of outlawry.

Religious differences cut deeply into some political structures. The partition of India had much the same separatist influence as would an attempt to partition the United States into Catholic America and Protestant America. The electoral register system—introduced by England into India—is used in Lebanon today. That nation is divided into Moslem, Druse, and Christian districts from which only a Moslem, a Druse, or a Christian respectively can be elected. The qualification for office is therefore a religious one, not a candidate's experience and general capabilities.

Hitler's idea of the master race is the foundation of *apartheid* in South Africa; and the fanatical Negroes who sponsor the Muslim League in America make the same claim to Black Supremacy. Racism is sometimes founded on economics. The Armenian, the Jew, the Greek, the Chinese is often despised by those who do not have the same acquisitive nature or ability. Those not so able in business and finance find themselves out of a job because of their astute competitors; or they may end up working for the persons who outdistance them in that kind of contest. The latter is true in Indonesia and Malaya, where the local people awakened to the fact that most of the wealth was owned by the Chinese. The hatred and suspicion that resulted are not peculiar to the rampant animosity that the browns often show toward the yellows. It explains a good deal of the anti-Semitism that has plagued the world. And, in the Fiji Islands, I learned that the local people hate the Indian landowners for much the same reason. At home, the unskilled white laborer often fears the competition of the Negro.

Racism, when openly discussed, is usually placed in terms of "superiority" versus "inferiority."

Even the anthropologists quarrel over those terms. At first glance, there may seem to be widespread racial differences. The Chinese, for example, who had to withstand severe winters and droughts, developed a resourcefulness that Malays living in a more benign environment did not need. But whether this was due to heredity or environment has never been proven.

In the United States, the major controversy has centered on the alleged difference between the Negro and the white. Those who would attempt to prove innate differences have relied chiefly on IQ tests and on their own ideas of what constitutes "civilization." The great majority of social scientists and physical anthropologists, however, agree that it is impossible to draw meaningful conclusions from tests which cannot take into account the very real cultural and environmental factors which have handicapped Ne-

groes taking those tests. Scores are significantly lower
where children have been educated in poorer schools,
or in states where less money is spent on the school
budget. Neither innate differences nor innate equality is capable of being proven—race by race.

There are those who would run the nation on a
basis of the proved achievements of one race. John C.
Calhoun, who advocated that theory, has modern followers. In theory, one would then have the Republic
of Plato, where instead of democracy, with each man
having an equal say in government, one would have
oligarchy: government by those innately fit to rule
over those innately fit to serve. This is the type of
government which Lincoln rejected. Today equality
must mean equality of education, of work, of opportunity to travel and to assimilate all aspects of the
world's cultures. The idea of "superior" and "inferior" races is usually a man-made distinction to serve
a political or social end, and misses the point of equal
opportunity to which Lincoln was dedicated.

Mr. Justice Holmes wrote in 1913:

". . . as I grow older I grow calm. If I feel what
are perhaps an old man's apprehensions, that competition from new races will cut deeper than working
men's disputes and will test whether we can hang
together and can fight; if I fear that we are running
through the world's resources at a pace that we cannot keep; I do not lose my hopes. I do not pin my
dreams for the future to my country or even to my
race. I think it probable that civilization somehow

will last as long as I care to look ahead—perhaps with smaller numbers, but perhaps also bred to greatness and splendor by science. I think it not improbable that man, like the grub that prepares a chamber for the winged thing it never has seen but is to be—that man may have cosmic destinies that he does not understand. And so beyond the vision of battling races and an impoverished earth I catch a dreaming glimpse of peace."

When two races are brought together in the same community, they in time either blend or one is eventually exterminated. Extermination was the fate of many aborigines in Australia. Settlers in Tasmania, for example, hunted down the aborigines as we hunted down wolves. None of the aborigines of Tasmania survived. Survival or amalgamation seems to be the fate of each race. It may be romantic to think of the future in terms of blue-eyed, fair-haired people. But it is not a reliable article of faith. As the years pass, the amalgamation of the races increases. Malays and Chinese—Negroes and whites—whites and browns—yellows and whites. The full-bloods among the American Indians steadily decrease. In Panama, where Indian, Spaniard, and Negro have lived for years, those without Negro blood are less than 10 percent.

The fear of racial amalgamation is the unstated premise of much of the opposition to integration of schools, parks, buses, trains, waiting rooms, and other public facilities. It has caused the phrase "with malice toward none" to be rewritten. Yet Lincoln's rejection of "malice" and his embrace of "charity" have a potent influence in the world even a century after his death.

"I shall do nothing in malice. What I deal with is too vast for malicious dealing."

Today he represents the democratic ideal to uncounted millions who have never known justice, who have never experienced equality. The most enduring monument a person can have, he once said, is not made of marble; it is "in the hearts of those who love liberty, unselfishly, for all men."

The underprivileged peoples of all continents have enshrined him in their hearts.

His symbol now is different from the one his deed and words warrant. In Africa especially he has become the champion of every black still denied first-class citizenship and equal justice under law.

# APPENDIX

# "*All men are created equal*"

PREAMBLE TO DECLARATION OF
INDEPENDENCE JULY 4, 1776

WHEN in the Course of human events, it becomes necessary for one people to dissolve the political bands which
have connected them with another, and to assume
among the Powers of the earth, the separate and equal
station to which the Laws of Nature and of Nature's
God entitle them, a decent respect to the opinions of
mankind requires that they should declare the causes
which impel them to the separation.

We hold these truths to be self-evident, that all men
are created equal, that they are endowed by their Creator with certain unalienable Rights, that among these
are Life, Liberty and the pursuit of Happiness. That
to secure these rights, Governments are instituted
among Men, deriving their just powers from the consent
of the governed, That whenever any Form of Government becomes destructive of these ends, it is the Right
of the People to alter or abolish it, and to institute new
Government, laying its foundation on such principles
and organizing its powers in such form, as to them shall
seem most likely to effect their Safety and Happiness.
Prudence, indeed, will dictate that Governments long
established should not be changed for light and tran-
sient causes; and accordingly all experience hath shown,

that mankind are more disposed to suffer, while evils are sufferable, than to right themselves by abolishing the forms to which they are accustomed. But when a long train of abuses and usurpations, pursuing invariably the same Object evinces a design to reduce them under absolute Despotism, it is their right, it is their duty, to throw off such Government, and to provide new Guards for their future security. . . .

# "Of the people, by the people, for the people"

GETTYSBURG ADDRESS

NOVEMBER 19, 1863

———

FOURSCORE and seven years ago our fathers brought forth on this continent a new nation, conceived in Liberty, and dedicated to the proposition that all men are created equal.

Now we are engaged in a great civil war, testing whether that nation, or any nation so conceived and so dedicated, can long endure. We are met on a great battlefield of that war. We have come to dedicate a portion of that field, as a final resting-place for those who here gave their lives that that nation might live. It is altogether fitting and proper that we should do this.

But, in a larger sense, we cannot dedicate—we cannot consecrate—we cannot hallow—this ground. The brave men, living and dead, who struggled here, have consecrated it far above our poor power to add or detract. The world will little note, nor long remember, what we say here, but it can never forget what they did here. It is for us the living, rather, to be dedicated here to the unfinished work which they who fought here have thus far so nobly advanced. It is rather for us to be here dedicated to the great task remaining before us—that from these honored dead we take increased devotion to that cause for which they gave the last full measure of devotion; that we here highly resolve that these dead shall not have died in vain; that this nation, under God, shall have a new birth of freedom; and that government of the people, by the people, for the people, shall not perish from the earth.

# "With malice toward none, with charity for all"

SECOND INAUGURAL

MARCH 4, 1865

FELLOW-COUNTRYMEN:

At this second appearing to take the oath of the presidential office, there is less occasion for an extended address than there was at the first. Then a statement, somewhat in detail, of a course to be pursued, seemed fitting and proper. Now, at the expiration of four years, during which public declarations have been constantly called forth on every point and phase of the great contest which still absorbs the attention and engrosses the energies of the nation, little that is new could be presented. The progress of our arms, upon which all else chiefly depends, is as well known to the public as to myself; and it is, I trust, reasonably satisfactory and encouraging to all. With high hope for the future, no prediction in regard to it is ventured.

On the occasion corresponding to this four years ago, all thoughts were anxiously directed to an impending civil war. All dreaded it—all sought to avert it. While the inaugural address was being delivered from this place, devoted altogether to *saving* the Union without war, insurgent agents were in the city seeking to *destroy* it without war—seeking to dissolve the Union, and divide effects, by negotiation. Both parties deprecated war; but one of them would *make* war rather than let the nation survive; and the other would *accept* war rather than let it perish. And the war came.

One-eighth of the whole population were colored slaves, not distributed generally over the Union, but localized in the Southern part of it. These slaves constituted a peculiar and powerful interest. All knew that this interest was, somehow, the cause of the war. To strengthen, perpetuate, and extend this interest was the object for which the insurgents would rend the Union, even by war; while the government claimed no right to do more than to restrict the territorial enlargement of it.

Neither party expected for the war the magnitude or the duration which it has already attained. Neither anticipated that the *cause* of the conflict might cease with, or even before, the conflict itself should cease. Each looked for an easier triumph, and a result less fundamental and astounding. Both read the same Bible, and pray to the same God; and each invokes His aid against the other. It may seem strange that any men should dare to ask a just God's assistance in wringing their bread from the sweat of other men's faces; but let us judge not, that we be not judged. The prayers of both could not be answered—that of neither has been answered fully.

The Almighty has His own purposes. "Woe unto the world because of offenses! for it must needs be that offenses come; but woe to that man by whom the offense cometh." If we shall suppose that American slavery is one of those offenses which, in the providence of God, must needs come, but which, having continued through his appointed time, he now wills to remove, and that he gives to both North and South this terrible war, as the woe due to those by whom the offense came, shall we discern therein any departure from those divine attributes which the believers in a living God always ascribe to him?

Fondly do we hope, fervently do we pray, that this mighty scourge of war may speedily pass away. Yet, if God wills that it continue until all the wealth piled by the bondsman's two hundred and fifty years of unrequited toil shall be sunk, and until every drop of blood drawn with the lash shall be paid by another drawn with the sword, as was said three thousand years ago, so still it must be said, "The judgments of the Lord are true and righteous altogether."

With malice toward none; with charity for all; with firmness in the right, as God gives us to see the right, let us strive on to finish the work we are in; to bind up the nation's wounds; to care for him who shall have borne the battle and for his widow, and his orphan— to do all which may achieve and cherish a just and lasting peace among ourselves, and with all nations.

# "Thenceforward and forever free"

EMANCIPATION PROCLAMATION

JANUARY 1, 1863

WHEREAS, on the twenty-second day of September, in the year of our Lord one thousand eight hundred and sixty-two, a proclamation was issued by the President of the United States, containing, among other things, the following, to wit:

"That on the first day of January, in the year of our Lord one thousand eight hundred and sixty-three, all persons held as slaves within any State or designated part of a State, the people whereof shall then be in rebellion against the United States, shall be then, thenceforward, and forever, free; and the Executive government of the United States, including the military and naval authority thereof, will recognize and maintain the freedom of such persons, and will do no act or acts to repress such persons, or any of them, in any efforts they may make for their actual freedom.

"That the Executive will, on the first day of January aforesaid, by proclamation, designate the States and parts of States, if any, in which the people thereof, respectively, shall then be in rebellion against the United States; and the fact that any State, or the people thereof, shall on that day be in good faith represented in the Congress of the United States, by members chosen thereto at elections wherein a majority of the qualified voters of such State shall have participated, shall, in the absence of strong countervailing testimony, be deemed conclusive evidence that such State, and the people thereof, are not then in rebellion against the United States."

Now, therefore, I, Abraham Lincoln, President of the United States, by virtue of the power in me vested as commander-in-chief of the army and navy of the United States, in time of actual armed rebellion against the authority and Government of the United States, and as a fit and necessary war measure for suppressing said rebellion, do, on this first day of January, in the year of our Lord one thousand eight hundred and sixty-three, and in accordance with my purpose so to do, publicly proclaimed for the full period of one hundred days from the first day above mentioned, order and designate as the States and parts of States wherein the people thereof, respectively, are this day in rebellion against the United States, the following, to wit:

Arkansas, Texas, Louisiana, (except the parishes of St. Bernard, Plaquemines, Jefferson, St. John, St. Charles, St. James, Ascension, Assumption, Terre Bonne, Lafourche, St. Mary, St. Martin, and Orleans, including the city of New Orleans), Mississippi, Alabama, Florida, Georgia, South Carolina, North Carolina, and Virginia, (except the forty-eight counties designated as West Virginia, and also the counties of Berkeley, Accomac, Northampton, Elizabeth City, York, Princess Ann, and Norfolk, including the cities of Norfolk and Portsmouth), and which excepted parts are for the present left precisely as if this proclamation were not issued.

And by virtue of the power and for the purpose aforesaid, I do order and declare that all persons held as slaves within said designated States and parts of States are and henceforward shall be free; and that the Executive government of the United States, including the military and naval authorities thereof, will recognize and maintain the freedom of said persons.

And I hereby enjoin upon the people so declared to be free to abstain from all violence, unless in necessary self-defense; and I recommend to them that, in all cases when allowed, they labor faithfully for reasonable wages.

And I further declare and make known that such persons, of suitable condition, will be received into the armed service of the United States, to garrison forts, positions, stations, and other places, and to man vessels of all sorts in said service.

And upon this act, sincerely believed to be an act of justice warranted by the Constitution upon military necessity, I invoke the considerate judgment of mankind and the gracious favor of Almighty God.

In witness whereof, I have hereunto set my hand and caused the seal of the United States to be affixed.

Done at the city of Washington this first day of January, in the year of our Lord one thousand eight hundred and sixty-three, and of the independence of the United States of America the eighty-seventh.

ABRAHAM LINCOLN

By the President:

William H. Seward, Secretary of State

# *Abolition of slavery, equal protection of the laws, and the right to vote*

THIRTEENTH AMENDMENT

DECEMBER 18, 1865

SECTION 1. Neither slavery nor involuntary servitude, except as a punishment for crime whereof the party shall have been duly convicted, shall exist within the United States, or any place subject to their jurisdiction.
SECTION 2. Congress shall have power to enforce this article by appropriate legislation.

FOURTEENTH AMENDMENT

JULY 28, 1868

SECTION 1. All persons born or naturalized in the United States, and subject to the jurisdiction thereof, are citizens of the United States and of the State wherein they reside. No State shall make or enforce any law which shall abridge the privileges or immunities of citizens of the United States; nor shall any State deprive any person of life, liberty, or property, without due process of law; nor deny to any person within its jurisdiction the equal protection of the laws.

SECTION 2. Representatives shall be apportioned among the several States according to their respective numbers, counting the whole number of persons in each State, excluding Indians not taxed. But when the right to vote at any election for the choice of electors for President and Vice-President of the United States, Representatives in Congress, the Executive and Judicial officers of a State, or the members of the Legislature thereof, is denied to any of the male inhabitants of such State, being twenty-one years of age, and citizens of the United States, or in any way abridged, except for participation in rebellion, or other crime, the basis of representation therein shall be reduced in the proportion which the number of such male citizens shall bear to the whole number of male citizens twenty-one years of age in such State.

SECTION 3. No person shall be a Senator or Representative in Congress, or elector of President and Vice-President, or hold any office, civil or military, under the United States, or under any State, who, having previously taken an oath, as a member of Congress, or as an officer of the United States, or as a member of any State legislature, or as an executive or judicial officer of any State, to support the Constitution of the United States, shall have engaged in insurrection or rebellion against the same, or given aid or comfort to the enemies thereof. But Congress may by a vote of two-thirds of each House, remove such disability.

SECTION 4. The validity of the public debt of the United States, authorized by law, including debts incurred for payment of pensions and bounties for services in suppressing insurrection or rebellion, shall not be questioned. But neither the United States nor any State shall assume or pay any debt or obligation incurred in aid of insurrection or rebellion against the United States, or any claim for the loss or emancipation of any slave; but all such debts, obligations and claims shall be held illegal and void.

SECTION 5. The Congress shall have power to enforce, by appropriate legislation, the provisions of this article.

## FIFTEENTH AMENDMENT
### MARCH 30, 1870

SECTION 1. The right of citizens of the United States to vote shall not be denied or abridged by the United States or by any State on account of race, color, or previous condition of servitude—

SECTION 2. The Congress shall have power to enforce this article by appropriate legislation.

# "Separate but equal"

PLESSY V. FERGUSON, 163 U.S. 537
ERROR TO THE SUPREME COURT OF THE
STATE OF LOUISIANA
DECIDED MAY 18, 1896

Mr. Justice Brown, after stating the case, delivered the opinion of the court.

This case turns upon the constitutionality of an act of the General Assembly of the State of Louisiana, passed in 1890, providing for separate railway carriages for the white and colored races. Acts 1890, No. 111, p. 152. . . .

The information filed in the criminal District Court charged in substance that Plessy, being a passenger between two stations within the State of Louisiana, was assigned by officers of the company to the coach used for the race to which he belonged, but he insisted upon going into a coach used by the race to which he did not belong. . . .

The constitutionality of this act is attacked upon the ground that it conflicts both with the Thirteenth Amendment of the Constitution, abolishing slavery, and the Fourteenth Amendment, which prohibits certain restrictive legislation on the part of the States.

1. That it does not conflict with the Thirteenth Amendment, which abolished slavery and involuntary servitude, except as a punishment for crime, is too clear

for argument. Slavery implies involuntary servitude—a state of bondage; the ownership of mankind as a chattel, or at least the control of the labor and services of one man for the benefit of another, and the absence of a legal right to the disposal of his own person, property and services. This amendment was said in the *Slaughterhouse cases,* 16 Wall. 36, to have been intended primarily to abolish slavery, as it had been previously known in this country, and that it equally forbade Mexican peonage or the Chinese coolie trade, when they amounted to slavery or involuntary servitude, and that the use of the word "servitude" was intended to prohibit the use of all forms of involuntary slavery, of whatever class or name. It was intimated, however, in that case that this amendment was regarded by the statesmen of that day as insufficient to protect the colored race from certain laws which had been enacted in the Southern States, imposing upon the colored race onerous disabilities and burdens, and curtailing their rights in the pursuit of life, liberty and property to such an extent that their freedom was of little value; and that the Fourteenth Amendment was devised to meet this exigency.

So, too, in the *Civil Rights cases,* 109 U.S. 3, 24, it was said that the act of a mere individual, the owner of an inn, a public conveyance or place of amusement, refusing accommodations to colored people, cannot be justly regarded as imposing any badge of slavery or servitude upon the applicant, but only as involving an ordinary civil injury, properly cognizable by the laws of the State, and presumably subject to redress by those laws until the contrary appears. "It would be running the slavery argument into the ground," said Mr. Justice Bradley, "to make it apply to every act or discrimination which a person may see fit to make as to the guests he will entertain, or as to the people he will take into his coach or cab or car, or admit to his concert or theatre, or deal with in other matters of intercourse or business."

A statute which implies merely a legal distinction between the white and colored races—a distinction which is founded in the color of the two races, and which must always exist so long as white men are distinguished from the other race by color—has no tendency to destroy the legal equality of the two races, or reestablish a state of involuntary servitude. Indeed, we do not understand that the Thirteenth Amendment is strenuously relied upon by the plaintiff in error in this connection.

2. By the Fourteenth Amendment, all persons born or naturalized in the United States, and subject to the jurisdiction thereof, are made citizens of the United States and of the State wherein they reside; and the States are forbidden from making or enforcing any law which shall abridge the privileges or immunities of citizens of the United States, or shall deprive any person of life, liberty or property without due process of law, or deny to any person within their jurisdiction the equal protection of the laws.

The proper construction of this amendment was first called to the attention of this court in the *Slaughterhouse cases,* 16 Wall. 36, which involved, however, not a question of race, but one of exclusive privileges. The case did not call for any expression of opinion as to the exact rights it was intended to secure to the colored race, but it was said generally that its main purpose was to establish the citizenship of the negro; to give definitions of citizenship of the United States and of the States, and to protect from the hostile legislation of the States the privileges and immunities of citizens of the United States, as distinguished from those of citizens of the States.

The object of the amendment was undoubtedly to enforce the absolute equality of the two races before the law, but in the nature of things it could not have been intended to abolish distinctions based upon color, or to enforce social, as distinguished from political equality, or a commingling of the two races upon terms unsatisfactory to either. Laws permitting, and even requiring, their separation in places where they are liable to be brought into contact do not necessarily imply the inferiority of either race to the other, and have been generally, if not universally, recognized as within the competency of the state legislatures in the exercise of their police power. The most common instance of this is connected with the establishment of separate schools for white and colored children, which has been held to be a valid exercise of the legislative power even by courts of the States where the political rights of the colored race have been longest and most earnestly enforced.

One of the earliest of these cases is that of *Roberts v. City of Boston,* 5 Cush. 198, in which the Supreme Judicial Court of Massachusetts held that the general school committee of Boston had power to make provisions for the instruction of colored children in separate schools established exclusively for them, and to prohibit their attendance upon the other schools. . . .

Laws forbidding the intermarriage of the two races may be said in a technical sense to interfere with the freedom of contract, and yet have been universally recognized as within the police power of the State. *State* v. *Gibson,* 36 Indiana, 389.

The distinction between laws interfering with the political equality of the negro and those requiring the separation of the two races in schools, theatres and railway carriages has been frequently drawn by this court. Thus in *Strauder* v. *West Virginia,* 100 U.S. 303, it was held that a law of West Virginia limiting to white male persons, 21 years of age and citizens of the State, the right to sit upon juries, was a discrimination which implied a legal inferiority in civil society, which lessened the security of the right of the colored race, and was a step toward reducing them to a condition of servility. Indeed, the right of a colored man that, in the selection of jurors to pass upon his life, liberty and property, there shall be no exclusion of his race, and no discrimination against them because of color, has been asserted in a number of cases. *Virginia* v. *Rives,* 100 U.S. 313; *Neale* v. *Delaware,* 103 U.S. 370; *Bush* v. *Kentucky,* 107 U.S. 110; *Gibson* v. *Mississippi,* 162 U.S. 565. So, where the laws of a particular locality of the charter of a particular railway corporation has provided that no person shall be excluded from the cars on account of color, we have held that this meant that persons of color should travel in the same car as white ones, and that the enactment was not satisfied by the company's providing cars assigned exclusively to people of color, though they were as good as those which they assigned exclusively to white persons. *Railroad Company* v. *Brown,* 17 Wall. 445.

Upon the other hand, where a statute of Louisiana required those engaged in the transportation of passengers among the States to give to all persons travelling within that State, upon vessels employed in that business, equal rights and privileges in all parts of the vessel, without distinction on account of race or color, and subjected to an action for damages the owner of such a vessel, who excluded colored passengers on account of their color from the cabin set aside by him for the use of whites, it was held to be so far as it applied to interstate commerce, unconstitutional and void. *Hall* v. *De Cuir,* 95 U.S. 485. The court in this case, however, expressly disclaimed that it had anything whatever to do with the statute as a regulation of internal commerce, or affecting anything else than commerce among the States. . . .

In the present case no question of interference with interstate commerce can possibly arise, since the East Louisiana Railway appears to have been purely a local line, with both its termini within the State of Louisiana. . . .

It is claimed by the plaintiff in error that, in any mixed community, the reputation of belonging to the dominant race, in this instance the white race, is *property,* in the same sense that a right of action, or of inheritance, is property. Conceding this to be so, for the purposes of this case, we are unable to see how this statute deprives him of, or in any way affects his right to, such property. If he be a white man and assigned to a colored coach, he may have his action for damages against the company for being deprived of his so called property. Upon the other hand, if he be a colored man and be so assigned, he has been deprived of no property, since he is not lawfully entitled to the reputation of being a white man.

In this connection, it is also suggested by the learned counsel for the plaintiff in error that the same argument that will justify the state legislature in requiring railways to provide separate accommodations for the two races will also authorize them to require separate cars to be provided for people whose hair is of a certain color, or who are aliens, or who belong to certain nationalities, or to enact laws requiring colored people to walk upon one side of the street, and white people upon the other, or requiring white men's horses to be painted white, and colored men's black, or their vehicles or business signs to be of different colors, upon the theory that one side of the street is as good as the other, or that a house or vehicle of one color is as good as one of another color. The reply to all this is that every exercise of the police power must be reasonable, and extend only to such laws as are enacted in good faith for the promotion of the public good, and not for the annoyance or oppression of a particular class. . . .

So far, then, as a conflict with the Fourteenth Amendment is concerned, the case reduces itself to the question whether the statute of Louisiana is a reasonable regulation, and with respect to this there must necessarily be a large discretion on the part of the legislature. In determining the question of reasonableness it is at liberty to act with reference to the established usages, customs and traditions of the people, and with a view to the promotion of their comfort, and the preservation of the public peace and good order. Gauged by this standard,

we cannot say that a law which authorizes or even requires the separation of the two races in public conveyances is unreasonable, or more obnoxious to the
Fourteenth Amendment than the acts of Congress requiring separate schools for colored children in the
District of Columbia, the constitutionality of which does
not seem to have been questioned, or the corresponding
acts of state legislatures. . . .

We consider the underlying fallacy of the plaintiff's
argument to consist in the assumption that the enforced
separation of the two races stamps the colored race with
a badge of inferiority. If this be so, it is not by reason
of anything found in the act, but solely because the
colored race chooses to put that construction upon it.
The argument necessarily assumes that if, as has been
more than once the case, and is not unlikely to be so
again, the colored race should become the dominant
power in the state legislature, and should enact a law in
precisely similar terms, it would thereby relegate the
white race to an inferior position. We imagine that the
white race, at least, would not acquiesce in this assumption. The argument also assumes that social prejudices
may be overcome by legislation, and that equal rights
cannot be secured to the negro except by an enforced
commingling of the two races. We cannot accept this
proposition. If the two races are to meet upon terms of
social equality, it must be the result of natural affinities,
a mutual appreciation of each other's merits and a voluntary consent of individuals . . . Legislation is power-
less to eradicate racial instincts or to abolish distinctions
based upon physical differences, and the attempt to do
so can only result in accentuating the difficulties of the

present situation. If the civil and political rights of both races be equal one cannot be inferior to the other civilly or politically. If one race be inferior to the other socially, the Constitution of the United States cannot put them upon the same plane.

It is true that the question of the proportion of colored blood necessary to constitute a colored person, as distinguished from a white person, is one upon which there is a difference of opinion in the different States, some holding that any visible admixture of black blood stamps the person as belonging to the colored race, (*State* v. *Chavers,* 5 Jones, [N.C.] 1, p. 11); others that it depends upon the preponderance of blood, (*Gray* v. *State,* 4 Ohio, 354; *Monroe* v. *Collins,* 17 Ohio St. 665); and still others that the predominance of white blood must only be in the proportion of three fourths. (*People* v. *Dean,* 14 Michigan, 406; *Jones* v. *Commonwealth,* 80 Virginia, 538). But these are questions to be determined under the laws of each State and are not properly put in issue in this case. Under the allegations of his petition it may undoubtedly become a question of importance whether, under the laws of Louisiana, the petitioner belongs to the white or colored race.

The judgment of the court below is, therefore,

*Affirmed.*

Mr. Justice Harlan dissenting.

By the Louisiana statute, the validity of which is here involved, all railway companies (other than street railroad companies) carrying passengers in that State are required to have separate but equal accommodations for white and colored persons, "by providing two or more passenger coaches for each passenger train, *or* by dividing the passenger coaches by a *partition* so as to secure separate accommodations." Under this statute, no colored person is permitted to occupy a seat in a coach assigned to white persons; nor any white person, to occupy a seat in a coach assigned to colored persons. The managers of the railroad are not allowed to exercise any discretion in the premises, but are required to assign each passenger to some coach or compartment set apart for the exclusive use of his race. If a passenger insists upon going into a coach or compartment not set apart for persons of his race, he is subject to be fined, or to be imprisoned in the parish jail. Penalties are prescribed for the refusal or neglect of the officers, directors, conductors and employes of railroad companies to comply with the provisions of the act.

Only "nurses attending children of the other race" are excepted from the operation of the statute. No exception is made of colored attendants travelling with adults. A white man is not permitted to have his colored servant with him in the same coach, even if his condition of health requires the constant, personal assistance of such servant. If a colored maid insists upon riding in the same coach with a white woman whom she has been employed to serve, and who may need her personal attention while travelling, she is subject to be fined or imprisoned for such an exhibition of zeal in the discharge of duty.

While there may be in Louisiana persons of different races who are not citizens of the United States, the words in the act, "white and colored races," necessarily include all citizens of the United States of both races residing in that State. So that we have before us a state enactment that compels, under penalties, the separation of the two races in railroad passenger coaches, and makes it a crime for a citizen of either race to enter a coach that has been assigned to citizens of the other race.

Thus the State regulates the use of a public highway by citizens of the United States solely upon the basis of race.

However apparent the injustice of such legislation may be, we have only to consider whether it is consistent with the Constitution of the United States.

That a railroad is a public highway, and that the corporation which owns or operates it is in the exercise of public functions, is not, at this day, to be disputed. . . .

In respect of civil rights, common to all citizens, the Constitution of the United States does not, I think, permit any public authority to know the race of those entitled to be protected in the enjoyment of such rights. Every true man has pride of race, and under appropriate circumstances when the rights of others, his equals before the law, are not to be affected, it is his privilege to express such pride and to take such action based upon it as to him seems proper. But I deny that any legislative body or judicial tribunal may have regard to the race of citizens when the civil rights of those citzens are involved. Indeed, such legislation, as that here in question, is inconsistent not only with that equality of rights which pertains to citizenship, National and State, but with the personal liberty enjoyed by every one within the United States.

The Thirteenth Amendment does not permit the withholding or the deprivation of any right necessarily

inhering in freedom. It not only struck down the institution of slavery as previously existing in the United
States, but it prevents the imposition of any burdens or
disabilities that constitute badges of slavery or servitude.
It decreed universal civil freedom in this country. This
court has so adjudged. But that amendment having been
found inadequate to the protection of the rights of those
who had been in slavery, it was followed by the Fourteenth Amendment, which added greatly to the dignity
and glory of American citizenship, and to the security
of personal liberty, by declaring that "all persons born
or naturalized in the United States, and subject to the
jurisdiction thereof, are citizens of the United States
and of the State wherein they reside," and that "no
State shall make or enforce any law which shall abridge
the privileges or immunities of citizens of the United
States; nor shall any State deprive any person of life,
liberty or property without due process of law, nor
deny to any person within its jurisdiction the equal protection of the laws." These two amendments, if enforced
according to their true intent and meaning, will protect
all the civil rights that pertain to freedom and citizenship. Finally, and to the end that no citizen should be
denied, on account of his race, the privilege of participating in the political control of his country, it was declared by the Fifteenth Amendment that "the right of
citizens of the United States to vote shall not be denied
or abridged by the United States or by any State on
account of race, color or previous condition of servitude."

These notable additions to the fundamental law were
welcomed by the friends of liberty throughout the

world. They removed the race line from our governmental systems. They had, as this court has said, a common purpose, namely, to secure "to a race recently emancipated, a race that through many generations have been held in slavery, all the civil rights that the superior race enjoy." They declared, in legal effect, this court has further said, "that the law in the States shall be the same for the black as for the white; that all persons, whether colored or white, shall stand equal before the laws of the States, and, in regard to the colored race, for whose protection the amendment was primarily designed, that no discrimination shall be made against them by law because of their color." We also said: "The words of the amendment, it is true, are prohibitory, but they contain a necessary implication of a positive immunity, or right, most valuable to the colored race —the right to exemption from unfriendly legislation against them distinctively as colored—exemption from legal discriminations, implying inferiority in civil society, lessening the security of their enjoyment of the rights which others enjoy, and discriminations which are steps towards reducing them to the condition of a subject race." It was, consequently, adjudged that a state law that excluded citizens of the colored race from juries, because of their race and however well qualified in other respects to discharge the duties of jurymen, was repugnant to the Fourteenth Amendment. *Strauder* v. *West Virginia,* 100 U.S. 303, 306, 307; *Virginia* v. *Rives,* 100 U.S. 313; *Ex parte Virginia,* 100 U.S. 339; *Neal* v. *Delaware,* 103 U.S. 370, 386; *Bush* v. *Kentucky,* 107 U.S. 110, 116. At the present term, referring to the previous adjudications, this court declared that "underlying all of those decisions is the principle that the Constitution of the United States, in its present form, forbids, so far as civil and political rights are concerned, discrimination by the General Government or the States against any citizen because of his race. All citizens are equal before the law." *Gibson* v. *Mississippi,* 162 U.S. 565.

The decisions referred to show the scope of the recent amendments of the Constitution. They also show that it is not within the power of a State to prohibit colored citizens, because of their race, from participating as jurors in the administration of justice.

It was said in argument that the statute of Louisiana does not discriminate against either race, but prescribes a rule applicable alike to white and colored citizens. But this argument does not meet the difficulty. Every one knows that the statute in question had its origin in the purpose, not so much to exclude white persons from railroad cars occupied by blacks, as to exclude colored people from coaches occupied by or assigned to white persons. Railroad corporations of Louisiana did not make discrimination among whites in the matter of accommodation for travellers. The thing to accomplish was, under the guise of giving equal accommodation for whites and blacks, to compel the latter to keep to themselves while travelling in railroad passenger coaches. No one would be so wanting in candor as to assert the contrary. The fundamental objection, therefore, to the statute is that it interferes with the personal freedom of citizens. "Personal liberty," it has been well said, "consists in the power of locomotion, of changing situation, or removing one's person to whatsoever places one's

own inclination may direct, without imprisonment or restraint, unless by due course of law." 1 Bl. Com. *134.
If a white man and a black man choose to occupy the
same public conveyance on a public highway, it is their
right to do so, and no government, proceeding alone on
grounds of race, can prevent it without infringing the
personal liberty of each.

It is one thing for railroad carriers to furnish, or to
be required by law to furnish, equal accommodations
for all whom they are under a legal duty to carry. It is
quite another thing for government to forbid citizens
of the white and black races from travelling in the same
public conveyance, and to punish officers of railroad
companies for permitting persons of the two races to
occupy the same passenger coach. If a State can prescribe, as a rule of civil conduct, that whites and blacks
shall not travel as passengers in the same railroad coach,
why may it not so regulate the use of the streets of its
cities and towns as to compel white citizens to keep on
one side of a street and black citizens to keep on the
other? Why may it not, upon like grounds, punish
whites and blacks who ride together in street cars or
in open vehicles on a public road or street? Why may it
not require sheriffs to assign whites to one side of a
court-room and blacks to the other? And why may it
not also prohibit the commingling of the two races in
the galleries of legislative halls or in public assemblages
convened for the consideration of the political questions
of the day? Further, if this statute of Louisiana is consistent with the personal liberty of citizens, why may
not the State require the separation in railroad coaches
of native and naturalized citizens of the United States,

or of Protestants and Roman Catholics?

The answer given at the argument to these questions was that regulations of the kind they suggest would be unreasonable, and could not, therefore, stand before the law. Is it meant that the determination of questions of legislative power depends upon the inquiry whether the statute whose validity is questioned is, in the judgment of the courts, a reasonable one, taking all the circumstances into consideration? A statute may be unreasonable merely because a sound public policy forbade its enactment. But I do not understand that the courts have anything to do with the policy or expediency of legislation. A statute may be valid, and yet, upon grounds of public policy, may well be characterized as unreasonable. Mr. Sedgwick correctly states the rule when he says that the legislative intention being clearly ascertained, "the courts have no other duty to perform than to execute the legislative will, without any regard to their views as to the wisdom or justice of the particular enactment." Stat. & Const. Constr. 324. There is a dangerous tendency in these latter days to enlarge the functions of the courts, by means of judicial interference with the will of the people as expressed by the legislature. Our institutions have the distinguishing characteristic that the three departments of government are coordinate and separate. Each must keep within the limits defined by the Constitution. And the courts best discharge their duty by executing the will of the lawmaking power, constitutionally expressed, leaving the results of legislation to be dealt with by the people through their representatives. Statutes must always have a reasonable construction. Sometimes they are to be construed strictly; sometimes, liberally, in order to carry out the legislative will. But however construed, the intent of the legislature is to be respected, if the particular statute in question is valid, although the courts, looking at the public interests, may conceive the statute to be both unreasonable and impolitic. If the power exists to enact a statute, that ends the matter so far as the courts are concerned. The adjudged cases in which statutes have been held to be void, because unreasonable, are those in which the means employed by the legislature were not at all germane to the end to which the legislature was competent.

The white race deems itself to be the dominant race in this country. And so it is, in prestige, in achievements, in education, in wealth and in power. So, I doubt not, it will continue to be for all time, if it remains true to its great heritage and holds fast to the principles of constitutional liberty. But in view of the Constitution, in the eye of the law, there is in this country no superior, dominant, ruling class of citizens. There is no caste here. Our Constitution is color-blind, and neither knows nor tolerates classes among citizens. In respect of civil rights, all citizens are equal before the law. The humblest in the peer of the most powerful. The law regards man as man, and takes no account of his surroundings or his color when his civil rights as guaranteed by the supreme law of the land are involved. It is, therefore, to be regretted that this high tribunal, the final expositor of the fundamental law of the land, has reached the conclusion that it is competent for a State to regulate the enjoyment by citizens of their civil rights solely upon the basis of race.

In my opinion, the judgment this day rendered will, in time, prove to be quite as pernicious as the decision made by this tribunal in the *Dred Scott case*. It was adjudged in that case that the descendants of Africans who were imported into this country and sold as slaves were not included nor intended to be included under the word "citizens" in the Constitution, and could not claim any of the rights and privileges which that instrument provided for and secured to citizens of the United States; that at the time of the adoption of the Constitution they were "considered as a subordinate and inferior class of beings, who had been subjugated by the dominant race, and, whether emancipated or not, yet remained subject to their authority, and had no rights or privileges but such as those who held the power and the government might choose to grant them." 19 How. 393, 404. The recent amendments of the Constitution, it was supposed, had eradicated these principles from our institutions. But it seems that we have yet, in some of the States, a dominant race—a superior class of citizens, which assumes to regulate the enjoyment of civil rights, common to all citizens, upon the basis of race. The present decision, it may well be apprehended, will not only stimulate aggressions, more or less brutal and irritating, upon the admitted rights of colored citizens, but will encourage the belief that it is possible, by means of state enactments, to defeat the beneficent purpose which the people of the United States had in view when they adopted the recent amendments of the Constitution, by one of which the blacks of this country were made citizens of the United States and of the States in which they respectively reside, and whose privileges and immunities, as citizens, the States are forbidden to abridge. Sixty millions of whites are in no danger from the presence here of eight millions of blacks. The destinies of the two races, in this country, are indissolubly linked together, and the interests of both require that the common government of all shall not permit the seeds of race hate to be planted under the sanction of law. What can more certainly arouse race hate, what more certainly create and perpetuate a feeling of distrust between these races, than state enactments, which, in fact, proceed on the ground that colored citizens are so inferior and degraded that they cannot be allowed to sit in public coaches occupied by white citizens? That, as all will admit, is the real meaning of such legislation as was enacted in Louisiana.

The sure guarantee of the peace and security of each race is the clear, distinct, unconditional recognition by our governments, National and State, of every right that inheres in civil freedom, and of the equality before the law of all citizens of the United States without regard to race. State enactments, regulating the enjoyment of civil rights, upon the basis of race, and cunningly devised to defeat legitimate results of the war, under the pretense of recognizing equality of rights, can have no other result than to render permanent peace impossible, and to keep alive a conflict of races, the continuance of which must do harm to all concerned. This question is not met by the suggestion that social equality cannot exist between the white and black races in this country. That argument, if it can be properly regarded as one, is scarcely worthy of consideration; for social equality no more exists between two races when travelling in a passenger coach or a public highway than when members of the same race sit by each other in a street car or in the jury box, or stand or sit with each other in a political assembly, or when they use in common the streets of a city or town, or when they are in the same room for the purpose of having their names placed on the registry of voters, or when they approach the ballot-box in order to exercise the high privilege of voting.

There is a race so different from our own that we do not permit those belonging to it to become citizens of the United States. Persons belonging to it are, with few exceptions, absolutely excluded from our country. I allude to the Chinese race. But by the statute in question, a Chinaman can ride in the same passenger coach with white citizens of the United States, while citizens of the black race in Louisiana, many of whom, perhaps, risked their lives for the preservation of the Union, who are entitled, by law, to participate in the political control of the State and nation, who are not excluded, by law or by reason of their race, from public stations of any kind, and who have all the legal rights that belong to white citizens, are yet declared to be criminals, liable to imprisonment, if they ride in a public coach occupied by citizens of the white race. It is scarcely just to say that a colored citizen should not object to occupying a public coach assigned to his own race. He does not object, nor, perhaps, would he object to separate coaches for his race, if his rights under the law were recognized. But he objects, and ought never to cease objecting to the proposition, that citizens of the white and black races can be adjudged criminals because they sit, or claim the right to sit, in the same public coach on a public highway.

The arbitrary separation of citizens, on the basis of race, while they are on a public highway, is a badge of servitude wholly inconsistent with the civil freedom and the equality before the law established by the Constitution. It cannot be justified upon any legal grounds.

If evils will result from the commingling of the two races upon public highways established for the benefit of all, they will be infinitely less than those that will surely come from state legislation regulating the enjoyment of civil rights upon the basis of race. We boast of the freedom enjoyed by our people above all other peoples. But it is difficult to reconcile that boast with a state of the law which, practically, puts the brand of servitude and degradation upon a large class of our fellow-citizens, our equals before the law. The thin disguise of "equal" accommodations for passengers in railroad coaches will not mislead any one, nor atone for the wrong this day done.

The result of the whole matter is, that while this court has frequently adjudged, and at the present term has recognized the doctrine, that a State cannot, consistently with the Constitution of the United States, prevent white and black citizens, having the required qualifications for jury service, from sitting in the same jury box, it is now solemnly held that a State may prohibit white and black citizens from sitting in the same passenger coach on a public highway, or may require that they be separated by a "partition," when in the same passenger coach. May it not now be reasonably expected that astute men of the dominant race, who affect to be disturbed at the possibility that the integrity of the white race may be corrupted, or that its supremacy will be imperilled, by contact on public highways with black people, will endeavor to procure statutes requiring white and black jurors to be separated in the jury box by a "partition," and that, upon retiring from the court room to consult as to their verdict, such partition, if it be a moveable one, shall be taken to their consultation room, and set up in such way as to prevent black jurors from coming too close to their brother jurors of the white race. If the "partition" used in the court room happens to be stationary, provision could be made for screens with openings through which jurors of the two races could confer as to their verdict without coming into personal contact with each other. I cannot see but that, according to the principles this day announced, such state legislation, although conceived in hostility to, and enacted for the purpose of humiliating citizens of the United States of a particular race, would be held to be consistent with the Constitution.

I do not deem it necessary to review the decisions of state courts to which reference was made in argument. Some, and the most important, of them are wholly inapplicable, because rendered prior to the adoption of the last amendments of the Constitution, when colored people had very few rights which the dominant race felt obliged to respect. Others were made at a time when public opinion, in many localities, was dominated by the institution of slavery; when it would not have been safe to do justice to the black man; and when, so far as the rights of blacks were concerned, race prejudice was, practically, the supreme law of the land. Those decisions cannot be guides in the era introduced by the recent amendments of the supreme law, which established universal civil freedom, gave citizenship to all born or naturalized in the United States and residing here, obliterated the race line from our systems of governments, National and State, and placed our free institutions upon the broad and sure foundation of the equality of all men before the law.

I am of opinion that the statute of Louisiana is inconsistent with the personal liberty of citizens, white and black, in that State, and hostile to both the spirit and letter of the Constitution of the United States. If laws of like character should be enacted in the several States of the Union, the effect would be in the highest degree mischievous. Slavery, as an institution tolerated by law would, it is true, have disappeared from our country, but there would remain a power in the States, by sinister legislation, to interfere with the full enjoyment of the blessings of freedom; to regulate civil rights, common to all citizens, upon the basis of race; and to place in a condition of legal inferiority a large body of American citizens, now constituting a part of the political community called the People of the United States, for whom, and by whom through representatives, our government is administered. Such a system is inconsistent with the guarantee given by the Constitution to each State of a republican form of government, and may be stricken down by Congressional action, or by the courts in the discharge of their solemn duty to maintain the supreme law of the land, anything in the constitution or laws of any State to the contrary notwithstanding.

For the reasons stated, I am constrained to withhold

my assent from the opinion and judgment of the majority.

Mr. Justice Brewer did not hear the argument or participate in the decision of this case.

# The right to vote

NIXON V. HERNDON

273 U.S., 536

DECIDED MARCH 7, 1927

Mr. Justice Holmes delivered the opinion of the Court.

This is an action against the Judges of Elections for refusing to permit the plaintiff to vote at a primary election in Texas. It lays the damages at five thousand dollars. The petition alleges that the plaintiff is a negro, a citizen of the United States and of Texas and a resident of El Paso, and in every way qualified to vote, as set forth in detail, except that the statute to be mentioned interferes with his right; that on July 26, 1924, a primary election was held at El Paso for the nomination of candidates for a senator and representatives in Congress and State and other offices, upon the Democratic ticket; that the plaintiff, being a member of the Democratic party, sought to vote but was denied the right by defendants; that the denial was based upon a Statute of Texas enacted in May, 1923, and designated Article 3093a, by the words of which "in no event shall a negro be eligible to participate in a Democratic party primary election held in the State of Texas," &c., and that this statute is contrary to the Fourteenth and Fifteenth Amendments to the Constitution of the United States. The de-

*154*

fendants moved to dismiss upon the ground that the subject matter of the suit was political and not within the jurisdiction of the Court and that no violation of the Amendments was shown. The suit was dismissed and a writ of error was taken directly to this Court. Here no argument was made on behalf of the defendants but a brief was allowed to be filed by the Attorney General of the State.

The objection that the subject matter of the suit is political is little more than a play upon words. Of course the petition concerns political action but it alleges and seeks to recover for private damage. That private damage may be caused by such political action and may be recovered for in a suit at law hardly has been doubted for over two hundred years, since *Ashby* v. *White,* 2 Ld. Raym. 938, 3 *id.* 320, and has been recognized by this Court. *Wiley* v. *Sinkler,* 179 U.S. 58, 64, 65. *Giles* v. *Harris,* 189 U.S. 475, 485. See also Judicial Code, §24 (11), (12), (14). Act of March 3, 1911, c. 231; 36 Stat. 1087, 1092. If the defendants' conduct was a wrong to the plaintiff the same reasons that allow a recovery for denying the plaintiff a vote at a final election allow it for denying a vote at the primary election that may determine the final result.

The important question is whether the statute can be sustained. But although we state it as a question the answer does not seem to us open to a doubt. We find it unnecessary to consider the Fifteenth Amendment, because it seems to us hard to imagine a more direct and obvious infringement of the Fourteenth. That Amendment, while it applies to all, was passed, as we know, with a special intent to protect the blacks from discrimination against them. *Slaughterhouse Cases,* 16 Wall. 36. *Strauder* v. *West Virginia,* 100 U.S. 303. That Amendment "not only gave citizenship and the privileges of citizenship to persons of color, but it denied to any State the power to withhold from them the equal protection of the laws. . . . What is this but declaring that the law in the States shall be the same for the black as for the white; that all persons, whether colored or white, shall stand equal before the laws of the States, and, in regard to the colored race, for whose protection the amendment was primarily designed, that no discrimination shall be made against them by law because of their color?" Quoted from the last case in *Buchanan* v. *Warley,* 245 U.S. 60, 77. See *Yick Wo* v. *Hopkins,* 118 U.S. 356, 374. The statute of Texas in the teeth of the prohibitions referred to assumes to forbid negroes to take part in a primary election the importance of which we have indicated, discriminating against them by the distinction of color alone. States may do a good deal of classifying that it is difficult to believe rational, but there are limits, and it is too clear for extended argument that color cannot be made the basis of statutory classification affecting the right set up in this case.

*Judgment reversed.*

# Discrimination in selection of juries

## AVERY V. GEORGIA
## 345 U.S. 559
### DECIDED MAY 25, 1953

═══════

MR. CHIEF JUSTICE VINSON delivered the opinion of the Court.

Petitioner was tried for rape in the Superior Court of Fulton County, Georgia. He was convicted and sentenced to death. The Supreme Court of Georgia affirmed after overruling petitioner's contention that the jury which convicted him had been selected by a means repugnant to the Equal Protection Clause of the Fourteenth Amendment. We granted certiorari to review this claim. 345 U.S. 903.

The indictment, upon which petitioner was tried, was returned by a grand jury in Walker County, Georgia. A change of venue was granted and the cause removed to Fulton County. By proper pleadings petitioner, a Negro, challenged the array of petit jurors selected to try his case; he charged that discrimination had been practiced against members of his race. Testimony was then taken, and thereafter the trial court overruled the challenge.

The salient facts, developed in this hearing, are undisputed. Under Georgia law the task of organizing panels of petit jurors for criminal cases falls upon a county Board of Jury Commissioners. In discharging this responsibility the Commissioners, at stated intervals, select prospective jurors from the county tax returns. Their list is then printed; the names of white persons on this list are printed on white tickets; the names of Negroes are printed on yellow tickets. These tickets—white and yellow—are placed in a jury box. A judge of the Superior Court then draws a number of tickets from the box. The tickets are handed to a sheriff who in turn entrusts them to a clerk. It is the clerk's duty to "arrange" the tickets and to type up, in final form, the list of persons to be called to serve on the panel.

Approximately sixty persons were selected to make up the panel from which the jury in this particular case was drawn. The judge who picked out the tickets—bearing the names of persons composing the panel—testified that he did not, nor had he ever, practiced discrimination in any way, in the discharge of that duty. There is no contradictory evidence. Yet the fact remains that there was not a single Negro in that panel. The State concedes that Negroes are available for jury service in Fulton County, and we are told that Negroes generally do serve on juries in the courts of that county. The question we must decide, based upon our independent analysis of the record, is whether petitioner has made a sufficient showing of discrimination in the organization of this particular panel. We think he has.

The Jury Commissioners, and the other officials responsible for the selection of this panel, were under a constitutional duty to follow a procedure—"a course of conduct"—which would not "operate to discriminate in the selection of jurors on racial grounds." *Hill* v. *Texas,* 316 U.S. 400, 404 (1942). If they failed in that duty, then this conviction must be reversed—no matter how strong the evidence of petitioner's guilt. That is the law established by decisions of this Court spanning more than seventy years of interpretation of the meaning of "equal protection."

Petitioner's charge of discrimination in the jury selection in this case springs from the Jury Commissioners' use of white and yellow tickets. Obviously that practice makes it easier for those to discriminate who are of a mind to discriminate. Further, the practice has no authorization in the Georgia statutes—which simply enjoin the Commissioners to select "upright and intelligent men to serve as jurors. . . ." It is important to note that the Supreme Court of Georgia, in this case, specifically disapproved of the use of separately colored tickets in Fulton County, saying that it constituted "prima facie evidence of discrimination."

We agree. Even if the white and yellow tickets were drawn from the jury box without discrimination, opportunity was available to resort to it at other stages in the selection process. And, in view of the case before us, where not a single Negro was selected to serve on a panel of sixty—though many were available—we think that petitioner has certainly established a prima facie case of discrimination.

The court below affirmed, however, because petitioner had failed to prove some particular act of discrimination by some particular officer responsible for the selection of the jury; and the State now argues that it is petitioner's burden to fill this "factual vacuum." We cannot agree. If there is a "vacuum" it is one which the State must fill, by moving in with sufficient evidence to dispel the prima facie case of discrimination. We have held before, and the Georgia Supreme Court, itself, recently followed these decisions, that when a prima facie case of discrimination is presented, the burden falls, forthwith, upon the State to overcome it. The State failed to meet this test.

*Reversed.*

Mr. Justice Black concurs in the result.

Mr. Justice Jackson took no part in the consideration or decision of this case.

Mr. Justice Reed, concurring.

I concur in the reversal. My concurrence is based on the undisputed facts presented by the record. The facts that make a prima facie case of discrimination in the selection of petitioner's jury are as follows. The population of Fulton County is 691,797. Negroes comprise 25% or 165,814. The tax receiver's digest from which the jury list is selected has 105,035 white citizens and 17,736 Negroes—14%. The jury list for the year in question had 20,509 white and 1,115 Negroes—5%. From that list a number, 150 to 200, were drawn for service on each of the divisions of the court. Evidently these were for a week or a term's service. The venire from which the trial jury for Avery was selected numbered 60. All were white.

These facts establish a prima facie case of discrimination which the record does not rebut.

Mr. Justice Frankfurter, concurring.

It is undisputed that the drawings here were made from a box containing white and colored slips dif-ferentiated according to racial lines, white for white veniremen and yellow for colored. The slips were indiscriminately placed in the box and were drawn from the box by a county court judge. There was testimony from a recent member of the county Board of Jury Commissioners that the use of these white and yellow slips was designed for purposes of racial discrimination, and it has not been shown that they could serve any other purpose. So far as the particular facts of this case are concerned, we may accept the testimony of the judge who drew the slips from the box as to the honesty of his purpose; that testimony does not refute the fact that there were opportunities to discriminate, as experience tells us there will inevitably be when such differentiating slips are used. In this case the opportunities are obvious, partly because the aperture in the box was sufficiently wide to make open to view the color of the slips and partly because of the subsequent use or abuse that could be made of the slips however fairly drawn. However that may be, opportunity for working of a discriminatory system exists whenever the mechanism for jury selection has a component part, such as the slips here, that differentiates between white and colored; such a mechanism certainly cannot be countenanced when a discriminatory result is reached. The stark resulting phenomenon here was that somehow or other, despite the fact that over 5% of the slips were yellow, no Negro got onto the panel of 60 jurors from which Avery's jury was selected. The mind of justice, not merely its eyes, would have to be blind to attribute such an occurrence to mere fortuity.

Accordingly, I concur in the judgment.

# Restrictive covenants

SHELLEY V. KRAEMER

334 U.S. 1

DECIDED MAY 3, 1948

MR. CHIEF JUSTICE VINSON delivered the opinion of the Court.

These cases present for our consideration questions relating to the validity of court enforcement of private agreements, generally described as restrictive covenants, which have as their purpose the exclusion of persons of designated race or color from the ownership or occupancy of real property. Basic constitutional issues of obvious importance have been raised.

The first of these cases comes to this Court on certiorari to the Supreme Court of Missouri. On February 16, 1911, thirty out of a total of thirty-nine owners of property fronting both sides of Labadie Avenue between Taylor Avenue and Cora Avenue in the city of St. Louis, signed an agreement, which was subsequently recorded, providing in part:

". . . the said property is hereby restricted to the use and occupancy for the term of Fifty (50) years from this date, so that it shall be a condition all the time and whether recited and referred to as [sic] not in subsequent conveyances and shall attach to the land as a condition precedent to the sale of the same, that hereafter no part of said property or any portion thereof shall be, for said term of Fifty-years, occupied by any person not of the Caucasian race, it being intended hereby to restrict the use of said property for said period of time against the occupancy as owners or tenants of any portion of said property for resident or other purpose by people of the Negro or Mongolian Race."

The entire district described in the agreement included fifty-seven parcels of land. The thirty owners who signed the agreement held title to forty-seven parcels, including the particular parcel involved in this case. At the time the agreement was signed, five of the parcels in the district were owned by Negroes. One of those had been occupied by Negro families since 1882, nearly thirty years before the restrictive agreement was executed. The trial court found that owners of seven out of nine homes on the south side of Labadie Avenue, within the restricted district and "in the immediate vicinity" of the premises in question, had failed to sign the restrictive agreement in 1911. At the time this action was brought, four of the premises were occupied by Negroes, and had been so occupied for periods ranging from twenty-three to sixty-three years. A fifth parcel had been occupied by Negroes until a year before this suit was instituted.

On August 11, 1945, pursuant to a contract of sale, petitioners Shelley, who are Negroes, for valuable consideration received from one Fitzgerald a warranty deed to the parcel in question. The trial court found that petitioners had no actual knowledge of the restrictive agreement at the time of the purchase. . . .

On October 9, 1945, respondents, as owners of other property subject to the terms of the restrictive covenant, brought suit in the Circuit Court of the City of St. Louis praying that petitioners Shelley be restrained from taking possession of the property and that judgment be entered divesting title out of petitioners Shelley and revesting title in the immediate grantor or in such other person as the court should direct. The trial court denied the requested relief on the ground that the restrictive agreement, upon which respondents based their action, had never become final and complete because it was the intention of the parties to that agreement that it was not to become effective until signed by all property owners in the district, and signatures of all the owners had never been obtained.

The Supreme Court of Missouri sitting *en banc* reversed and directed the trial court to grant the relief for which respondents had prayed. That court held the agreement effective and concluded that enforcement of its provisions violated no rights guaranteed to petitioners by the Federal Constitution. At the time the court rendered its decision, petitioners were occupying the property in question.

The second of the cases under consideration comes to this Court from the Supreme Court of Michigan. The circumstances presented do not differ materially from the Missouri case. In June, 1934, one Ferguson and his wife, who then owned the property located in the city of Detroit which is involved in this case, executed a contract providing in part:

"This property shall not be used or occupied by any person or persons except those of the Caucasian race.

"It is further agreed that this restriction shall not be effective unless at least eighty percent of the property fronting on both sides of the street in the block where our land is located is subjected to this or a similar restriction."

The agreement provided that the restrictions were to remain in effect until January 1, 1960. The contract was subsequently recorded; and similar agreements were executed with respect to eighty percent of the lots in the block in which the property in question is situated.

By deed dated November 30, 1944, petitioners, who were found by the trial court to be Negroes, acquired title to the property and thereupon entered into its occupancy. On January 30, 1945, respondents, as owners of property subject to the terms of the restrictive agreement, brought suit against petitioners in the Circuit Court of Wayne County. After a hearing, the court entered a decree directing petitioners to move from the property within ninety days. Petitioners were further enjoined and restrained from using or occupying the premises in the future. On appeal, the Supreme Court of Michigan affirmed, deciding adversely to petitioners' contentions that they had been denied rights protected by the Fourteenth Amendment.

Petitioners have placed primary reliance on their contentions, first raised in the state courts, that judicial enforcement of the restrictive agreements in these cases has violated rights guaranteed to petitioners by the

Fourteenth Amendment of the Federal Constitution and Acts of Congress passed pursuant to that Amendment. Specifically, petitioners urge that they have been denied the equal protection of the laws, deprived of property without due process of law, and have been denied privileges and immunities of citizens of the United States. We pass to a consideration of those issues.

Whether the equal protection clause of the Fourteenth Amendment inhibits judicial enforcement by state courts of restrictive covenants based on race or color is a question which this Court has not heretofore been called upon to consider. * * *

It is well, at the outset, to scrutinize the terms of the restrictive agreements involved in these cases. In the Missouri case, the covenant declares that no part of the affected property shall be "occupied by any person not of the Caucasian race, it being intended hereby to restrict the use of said property . . . against the occupancy as owners or tenants of any portion of said property for resident or other purpose by people of the Negro or Mongolian Race." Not only does the restriction seek to proscribe use and occupancy of the affected properties by members of the excluded class, but as construed by the Missouri courts, the agreement requires that title of any person who uses his property in violation of the restriction shall be divested. The restriction of the covenant in the Michigan case seeks to bar occupancy by persons of the excluded class. It provides that "This property shall not be used or occupied by any person or persons except those of the Caucasian race."

It should be observed that these covenants do not seek to proscribe any particular use of the affected

properties. Use of the properties for residential occupancy, as such, is not forbidden. The restrictions of
these agreements, rather, are directed toward a designated class of persons and seek to determine who may
and who may not own or make use of the properties
for residential purposes. The excluded class is defined
wholly in terms of race or color; "simply that and nothing more."

It cannot be doubted that among the civil rights intended to be protected from discriminatory state action
by the Fourteenth Amendment are the rights to acquire,
enjoy, own and dispose of property. Equality in the enjoyment of property rights was regarded by the framers
of that Amendment as an essential precondition to the
realization of other basic civil rights and liberties which
the Amendment was intended to guarantee.

* * * *It is likewise clear that restrictions on the
right of occupancy of the sort sought to be created by
the private agreements in these cases could not be
squared with the requirements of the Fourteenth
Amendment if imposed by state statute or local ordinance. We do not understand respondents to urge the
contrary. In the case of *Buchanan* v. *Warley* (245 U.S.
60), a unanimous Court declared unconstitutional the
provisions of a city ordinance which denied to colored
persons the right to occupy houses in blocks in which
the greater number of houses were occupied by white
persons, and imposed similar restrictions on white persons with respect to blocks in which the greater number
of houses were occupied by colored persons. During the
course of the opinion in that case, this Court stated:
"The Fourteenth Amendment and these statutes en-

acted in furtherance of its purpose operate to qualify and entitle a colored man to acquire property without state legislation discriminating against him solely because of color."

In *Harmon* v. *Tyler,* 273 U.S. 668 (1927), a unanimous court, on the authority of *Buchanan* v. *Warley, supra,* declared invalid an ordinance which forbade any Negro to establish a home on any property in a white community or any white person to establish a home in a Negro community, "except on the written consent of a majority of the persons of the opposite race inhabiting such community or portion of the City to be affected."

The precise question before this Court in both the *Buchanan* and *Harmon* cases involved the rights of white sellers to dispose of their properties free from restrictions as to potential purchasers based on considerations of race or color. But that such legislation is also offensive to the rights of those desiring to acquire and occupy property and barred on grounds of race or color is clear, not only from the language of the opinion in *Buchanan* v. *Warley, supra,* but from this Court's disposition of the case of *Richmond* v. *Deans,* 281 U.S. 704 (1930). There, a Negro, barred from the occupancy of certain property by the terms of an ordinance similar to that in the *Buchanan* case, sought injunctive relief in the federal courts to enjoin the enforcement of the ordinance on the grounds that its provisions violated the terms of the Fourteenth Amendment. Such relief was granted, and this Court affirmed, finding the citation of *Buchanan* v. *Warley, supra,* and *Harmon* v. *Tyler, supra,* sufficient to support its judgment.

But the present cases, unlike those just discussed, do not involve action by state legislatures or city councils. Here the particular patterns of discrimination and the areas in which the restrictions are to operate, are determined, in the first instance, by the terms of agreements among private individuals. Participation of the State consists in the enforcement of the restrictions so defined. The crucial issue with which we are here confronted is whether this distinction removes these cases from the operation of the prohibitory provisions of the Fourteenth Amendment.

Since the decision of this Court in the *Civil Rights Cases,* 109 U.S. 3 (1883), the principle has become firmly embedded in our constitutional law that the action inhibited by the first section of the Fourteenth Amendment is only such action as may fairly be said to be that of the States. That Amendment erects no shield against merely private conduct, however discriminatory or wrongful.

We conclude, therefore, that the restrictive arguments standing alone cannot be regarded as violative of any rights guaranteed to petitioners by the Fourteenth Amendment. So long as the purposes of those agreements are effectuated by voluntary adherence to their terms, it would appear clear that there has been no action by the State and the provisions of the Amendment have not been violated. Cf. *Corrigan* v. *Buckley, supra.*

But here there was more. These are cases in which the purposes of the agreements were secured only by judicial enforcement by state courts of the restrictive terms of the agreements. The respondents urge that judicial enforcement of private agreements does not amount to state action; or, in any event, the participation of the States is so attenuated in character as not to amount to state action within the meaning of the Fourteenth Amendment. Finally, it is suggested, even if the States in these cases may be deemed to have acted in the constitutional sense, their action did not deprive petitioners of rights guaranteed by the Fourteenth Amendment. We move to a consideration of these matters.

That the action of state courts and judicial officers in their official capacities is to be regarded as action of the State within the meaning of the Fourteenth Amendment, is a proposition which has long been established by decisions of this Court. That principle was given expression in the earliest cases involving the construction of the terms of the Fourteenth Amendment. Thus, in *Virginia* v. *Rives,* 100 U.S. 313, 318 (1880), this Court stated: "It is doubtless true that a State may act through different agencies,—either by its legislative, its executive, or its judicial authorities; and the prohibitions of the amendment extend to all action of the State denying equal protection of the laws, whether it be action by one of these agencies or by another." In *Ex parte Virginia,* 100 U.S. 339, 347 (1880), the Court observed: "A State acts by its legislative, its executive, or its judicial authorities. It can act in no other way." In the *Civil Rights Cases,* 109 U.S. 3, 11, 17 (1883), this Court pointed out that the Amendment makes void "State action of every kind" which is inconsistent with the guaranties therein contained, and extends to manifestations of "State authority in the shape of laws, customs, or judicial or executive proceedings." Language to like effect is employed no less than eighteen times during the course of that opinion.

Similar expressions, giving specific recognition to the fact that judicial action is to be regarded as action of the State of the purposes of the Fourteenth Amendment, are to be found in numerous cases which have been more recently decided. In *Twining* v. *New Jersey*, 211 U.S. 78, 90-91 (1908), the Court said: "The judicial act of the highest court of the State, in authoritatively construing and enforcing its laws, is the act of the State." In *Brinkerhoff-Faris Trust & Savings Co.* v. *Hill*, 281 U.S. 673, 680 (1930), the Court, through Mr. Justice Brandeis, stated: "The federal guaranty of due process extends to state action through its judicial as well as through its legislative, executive or administrative branch of government." Further examples of such declarations in the opinions of this Court are not lacking.

One of the earliest applications of the prohibitions contained in the Fourteenth Amendment to action of state judicial officials occurred in cases in which Negroes had been excluded from jury service in criminal prosecutions by reason of their race or color. These cases demonstrate, also, the early recognition by this Court that state action in violation of the Amendment's provisions is equally repugnant to the constitutional commands whether directed by state statute or taken by a judicial official in the absence of statute. Thus, in *Strauder* v. *West Virginia*, 100 U.S. 303 (1880), this Court declared invalid a state statute restricting jury service to white persons as amounting to a denial of the equal protection of the laws to the colored defendant in that case. In the same volume of the reports, the Courts in *Ex parte Virginia, supra,* held that a similar discrimination imposed by the action of a state judge denied rights protected by the Amendment, despite the fact that the language of the state statute relating to jury service contained no such restrictions.

The action of state courts in imposing penalties or depriving parties of other substantive rights without providing adequate notice and opportunity to defend, has, of course, long been regarded as a denial of the due process of law guaranteed by the Fourteenth Amendment. *Brinkerhoff-Faris Trust & Savings Co.* v. *Hill, supra.* Cf. *Pennoyer* v. *Neff,* 95 U.S. 714 (1878).

In numerous cases, this Court has reversed criminal convictions in state courts for failure of those courts to provide the essential ingredients of a fair hearing. Thus it has been held that convictions obtained in state courts under the domination of a mob are void. *Moore* v. *Dempsey,* 261 U.S. 86 (1923). And see *Frank* v. *Mangum,* 237 U.S. 309 (1915). Convictions obtained by coerced confessions, by the use of perjured testimony known by the prosecution to be such, or without the effective assistance of counsel, have also been held to be exertions of state authority in conflict with the fundamental rights protected by the Fourteenth Amendment.

But the examples of state judicial action which have been held by this Court to violate the Amendment's commands are not restricted to situations in which the judicial proceedings were found in some manner to be procedurally unfair. It has been recognized that the action of state courts in enforcing a substantive common-law rule formulated by those courts, may result in the denial of rights guaranteed by the Fourteenth Amendment, even though the judicial proceedings in such cases may have been in complete accord with the most rigorous conceptions of procedural due process. Thus, in *American Federation of Labor* v. *Swing,* 312 U.S. 321 (1941), enforcement by state courts of the common-law policy of the State, which resulted in the restraining of peaceful picketing, was held to be state action of the sort prohibited by the Amendment's guaranties of freedom of discussion. In *Cantwell* v. *Connecticut,* 310 U.S. 296 (1940), a conviction in a state court of the common-law crime of breach of the peace was, under the circumstances of the case, found to be a violation of the Amendment's commands relating to freedom of religion. In *Bridges* v. *California,* 314 U.S. 252 (1941), enforcement of the state's common-law ruling relating to contempts by publication was held to be state action inconsistent with the prohibitions of the Fourteenth Amendment. And cf. *Chicago, Burlington and Quincy R. Co.* v. *Chicago,* 166 U.S. 226 (1897).

The short of the matter is that from the time of the adoption of the Fourteenth Amendment until the present, it has been the consistent ruling of this Court that the action of the States to which the Amendment has reference includes action of state courts and state judicial officials. Although, in construing the terms of the Fourteenth Amendment, differences have from time to time been expressed as to whether particular types of state action may be said to offend the Amendment's prohibitory provisions, it has never been suggested that state court action is immunized from the operation of those provisions simply because the act is that of the judicial branch of the state government.

Against this background of judicial construction, extending over a period of some three-quarters of a century, we are called upon to consider whether enforcement by state courts of the restrictive agreements in these cases may be deemed to be the acts of those States; and, if so, whether that action has denied these petitioners the equal protection of the laws which the Amendment was intended to insure.

We have no doubt that there has been state action in these cases in the full and complete sense of the phrase. The undisputed facts disclose that petitioners were willing purchasers of properties upon which they desired to establish homes. The owners of the properties were willing sellers; and contracts of sale were accordingly consummated. It is clear that but for the active intervention of the state courts, supported by the full panoply of state power, petitioners would have been free to occupy the properties in question without restraint.

These are not cases, as has been suggested, in which the States have merely abstained from action, leaving private individuals free to impose such discriminations as they see fit. Rather, these are cases in which the States have made available to such individuals the full coercive power of government to deny to petitioners, on the grounds of race or color, the enjoyment of property rights in premises which petitioners are willing and financially able to acquire and which the grantors are willing to sell. The difference between judicial enforcement and non-enforcement of the restrictive covenants is the difference to petitioners between being denied rights of property available to other members of the community and being accorded full enjoyment of those rights on an equal footing.

The enforcement of the restrictive agreements by the state courts in these cases was directed pursuant to the common-law policy of the States as formulated by those courts in earlier decisions. In the Missouri case, enforcement of the covenant was directed in the first instance by the highest court of the State after the trial court had determined the agreement to be invalid for want of the requisite number of signatures. In the Michigan case, the order of enforcement by the trial court was affirmed by the highest state court. The judicial action in each case bears the clear and unmistakable imprimatur of the State. We have noted that previous decisions of this Court have established the proposition that judicial action is not immunized from the operation of the Fourteenth Amendment simply because it is taken pursuant to the State's common-law policy. Nor is the Amendment ineffective simply because the particular pattern of discrimination, which the State has enforced, was defined initially by the terms of a private agreement. State action, as that phrase is understood for the purposes of the Fourteenth Amendment, refers to exertions of state power in all forms. And when the effect of that action is to deny rights subject to the protection of the Fourteenth Amendment, it is the obligation of this Court to enforce the constitutional demands.

We hold that in granting judicial enforcement of the restrictive agreements in these cases, the States have denied petitioners the equal protection of the laws and that, therefore, the action of the state courts cannot stand. We have noted that freedom from discrimination

*176*

by the States in the enjoyment of property rights was among the basic objectives sought to be effectuated by the framers of the Fourteenth Amendment. That such discrimination has occurred in these cases is clear. Because of the race or color of these petitioners they have been denied rights of ownership or occupancy enjoyed as a matter of course by other citizens of different race or color. The Fourteenth Amendment declares "that all persons, whether colored or white, shall stand equal before the laws of the States, and, in regard to the colored race, for whose protection the amendment was primarily designed, that no discrimination shall be made against them by law because of their color." *Strauder* v. *West Virginia, supra* at 307. Only recently this Court had occasion to declare that a state law which denied equal enjoyment of property rights to a designated class of citizens of specified race and ancestry, was not a legitimate exercise of the state's police power but violated the guaranty of the equal protection of the laws. *Oyama* v. *California,* 332 U.S. 633 (1948). Nor may the discriminations imposed by the state courts in these cases be justified as proper exertions of state police power. Cf. *Buchanan* v. *Warley, supra.*

Respondents urge, however, that since the state courts stand ready to enforce restrictive covenants excluding white persons from the ownership and occupancy of property covered by such agreements, enforcement of covenants excluding colored persons may not be deemed a denial of equal protection of the laws to the colored persons who are thereby affected. This contention does not bear scrutiny. The parties have directed our attention to no case in which a court, state or federal, has been called upon to enforce a covenant excluding members of the white majority from ownership or occupancy of real property on grounds of race or color. But there are more fundamental considerations. The rights created by the first section of the Fourteenth Amendment are, by its terms, guaranteed to the individual. The rights established are personal rights. It is, therefore, no answer to these petitioners to say that the courts may also be induced to deny white persons rights of ownership and occupancy on grounds of race or color. Equal protection of the laws is not achieved through indiscriminate imposition of inequalities.

Nor do we find merit in the suggestion that property owners who are parties to these agreements are denied equal protection of the laws if denied access to the courts to enforce the terms of restrictive covenants and to assert property rights which the state courts have held to be created by such agreements. The Constitution confers upon no individual the right to demand action by the State which results in the denial of equal protection of the laws to other individuals. And it would appear beyond question that the power of the State to create and enforce property interests must be exercised within the boundaries defined by the Fourteenth Amendment. Cf. *Marsh* v. *Alabama,* 326 U.S. 501 (1946).

The problem of defining the scope of the restrictions which the Federal Constitution imposes upon exertions of power by the States has given rise to many of the most persistent and fundamental issues which this Court has been called upon to consider. That problem was foremost in the minds of the framers of the Constitution, and, since that early day, has arisen in a multitude of forms. The task of determining whether the action of a State offends constitutional provisions is one which may not be undertaken lightly. Where, however, it is clear that the action of the State violates the terms of the fundamental charter, it is the obligation of this Court so to declare.

The historical context in which the Fourteenth Amendment became a part of the Constitution should not be forgotten. Whatever else the framers sought to achieve, it is clear that the matter of primary concern was the establishment of equality in the enjoyment of basic civil and political rights and the preservation of those rights from discriminatory action on the part of the States based on considerations of race or color. Seventy-five years ago this Court announced that the provisions of the Amendment are to be construed with this fundamental purpose in mind. Upon full consideration, we have concluded that in these cases the States have acted to deny petitioners the equal protection of the laws guaranteed by the Fourteenth Amendment. Having so decided, we find it unnecessary to consider whether petitioners have also been deprived of property without due process of law or denied privileges and immunities of citizens of the United States.

For the reasons stated, the judgment of the Supreme Court of Missouri and the judgment of the Supreme Court of Michigan must be reversed.

*Reversed.*

Mr. Justice Reed, Mr. Justice Jackson, and Mr. Justice Rutledge took no part in the consideration or decision of these cases.

# Segregation and equal protection

BROWN V. BOARD OF EDUCATION OF TOPEKA

347 U.S. 483

DECIDED MAY 17, 1954

MR. CHIEF JUSTICE WARREN delivered the opinion of the Court.

These cases come to us from the State of Kansas, South Carolina, Virginia, and Delaware. They are premised on different facts and different local conditions, but a common legal question justifies their consideration together in this consolidated opinion.

In each of the cases, minors of the Negro race through their legal representatives, seek the aid of the courts in obtaining admission to the public schools of their community on a nonsegregated basis. In each instance, they had been denied admission to schools attended by white children under laws requiring or permitting segregation according to race. This segregation was alleged to deprive the plaintiffs of the equal protection of the laws under the Fourteenth Amendment. In each of the cases other than the Delaware case, a three-judge federal district court denied relief to the plaintiffs on the so-called "separate but equal" doctrine announced by this Court in *Plessy* v. *Ferguson,* 163 U.S. 537. Under that doctrine, equality of treatment is accorded when the races are provided substantially equal facilities, even though these facilities be separate. In the Delaware case, the Supreme Court of Delaware adhered to that doctrine, but ordered that the plaintiffs be admitted to the white schools because of their superiority to the Negro schools.

The plaintiffs contend that segregated public schools are not "equal" and cannot be made "equal," and that hence they are deprived of the equal protection of the laws. Because of the obvious importance of the question presented, the Court took jurisdiction. Argument was heard in the 1952 Term, and reargument was heard this Term on certain questions propounded by the Court.

Reargument was largely devoted to the circumstances surrounding the adoption of the Fourteenth Amendment in 1868. It covered exhaustively consideration of the Amendment in Congress, ratification by the states, then existing practices in racial segregation, and the views of proponents and opponents of the Amendment. This discussion and our own investigation convinces us that, although these sources cast some light, it is not enough to resolve the problem with which we are faced. At best, they are inconclusive. The most avid proponents of the post-War Amendments undoubtedly intended them to remove all legal distinctions among "all persons born or naturalized in the United States." Their opponents, just as certainly, were antagonistic to both the letter and the spirit of the Amendments and wished them to have the most limited effect. What others in Congress and the state legislatures had in mind cannot be determined with any degree of certainty.

An additional reason for the inconclusive nature of the Amendment's history, with respect to segregated schools, is the status of public education at that time. In the South, the movement toward free common schools, supported by general taxation, had not yet taken hold. Education of white children was largely in the hands of private groups. Education of Negroes was almost nonexistent, and practically all of the race were illiterate. In fact, any education of Negroes was forbidden by law in some states. Today, in contrast, many Negroes have achieved outstanding success in the arts and sciences as well as in the business and professional world. It is true that public school education at the time of the Amendment had advanced further in the North, but the effect of the Amendment on Northern States was generally ignored in the congressional debates. Even in the North, the conditions of public education did not approximate those existing today. The curriculum was usually rudimentary; ungraded schools were common in rural areas; the school term was but three months a year in many states; and compulsory school attendance was virtually unknown. As a consequence, it is not surprising that there should be so little in the history of the Fourteenth Amendment relating to its intended effect on public education.

In the first cases in this Court construing the Fourteenth Amendment, decided shortly after its adoption, the Court interpreted it as proscribing all state-imposed discriminations against the Negro race. The doctrine of "separate but equal" did not make its appearance in this Court until 1896 in the case of *Plessy* v. *Ferguson, supra,* involving not education but transportation. American courts have since labored with the doctrine for over half a century. In this Court, there have been six cases involving the "separate but equal" doctrine in the field of public education. In *Cumming* v. *County Board of Education,* 175 U.S. 528, and *Gong Lum* v. *Rice,* 275 U.S. 78, the validity of the doctrine itself was not challenged. In more recent cases, all on the graduate school level, inequality was found in that specific benefits enjoyed by white students were denied to Negro students of the same educational qualifications. *Missouri ex rel. Gaines* v. *Canada,* 305 U.S. 337; *Sipuel* v. *Oklahoma,* 332 U.S. 631; *Sweatt* v. *Painter,* 339 U.S. 629; *McLaurin* v. *Oklahoma State Regents,* 339 U.S. 637. In none of these cases was it necessary to re-examine the doctrine to grant relief to the Negro plaintiff. And in *Sweatt* v. *Painter, supra,* the Court expressly reserved decision on the question whether *Plessy* v. *Ferguson* should be held inapplicable to public education.

In the instant cases, that question is directly presented. Here, unlike *Sweatt* v. *Painter,* there are findings below that the Negro and white schools involved have been equalized, or are being equalized, with respect to buildings, curricula, qualifications and salaries to teachers, and other "tangible" factors. Our decision, therefore, cannot turn on merely a comparison of these tangible factors in the Negro and white schools involved in each of the cases. We must look instead to the effect of segregation itself on public education.

In approaching this problem, we cannot turn the clock back to 1868 when the Amendment was adopted, or even to 1896 when *Plessy* v. *Ferguson* was written. We must consider public education in the light of its full development and its present place in American life throughout the Nation. Only in this way can it be determined if segregation in public schools deprives these plaintiffs of the equal protection of the laws.

Today, education is perhaps the most important function of state and local governments. Compulsory school attendance laws and the great expenditures for education both demonstrate our recognition of the importance of education to our democratic society. It is required in the performance of our most basic public responsibilities, even service in the armed forces. It is the very foundation of good citizenship. Today it is a principal instrument in awakening the child to cultural values, in preparing him for later professional training, and in helping him to adjust normally to his environment. In these days, it is doubtful that any child may reasonably be expected to succeed in life if he is denied the opportunity of an education. Such an opportunity, where the state has undertaken to provide it, is a right which must be made available to all on equal terms.

We come then to the question presented: Does segregation of children in public schools solely on the basis of race, even though the physical facilities and other "tangible" factors may be equal, deprive the children of the minority group of equal educational opportunities? We believe that it does.

In *Sweatt* v. *Painter, supra,* in finding that a segregated law school of Negroes could not provide them equal educational opportunities, this Court relied in large part on "those qualities which are incapable of objective measurement but which make for greatness in a law school." In *McLaurin* v. *Oklahoma State Regents, supra,* the Court, in requiring that a Negro admitted to a white graduate school be treated like all

*184*

other students, again resorted to intangible considerations: ". . . his ability to study, to engage in discussions and exchange views with other students, and, in general, to learn his profession." Such considerations apply with added force to children in grade and high schools. To separate them from others of similar age and qualifications solely because of their race generates a feeling of inferiority as to their status in the community that may affect their hearts and minds in a way unlikely ever to be undone. The effect of this separation on their educational opportunities was well stated by a finding in the Kansas case by a court which nevertheless felt compelled to rule against the Negro plaintiffs:

"Segregation of white and colored children in public schools has a detrimental effect upon the colored children. The impact is greater when it has the sanction of the law; for the policy of separating the races is usually interpreted as denoting the inferiority of the negro group. A sense of inferiority affects the motivation of a child to learn. Segregation with the sanction of law, therefore, has a tendency to [retard] the educational and mental development of negro children and to deprive them of some of the benefits they would receive in a racial[ly] integrated school system." Whatever may have been the extent of psychological knowledge at the time of *Plessy* v. *Ferguson,* this finding is amply supported by modern authority. Any language in *Plessy* v. *Ferguson* contrary to this finding is rejected.

We conclude that in the field of public education the doctrine of "separate but equal" has no place. Separate educational facilities are inherently unequal. Therefore, we hold that the plaintiffs and others similarly situated for whom the actions have been brought are, by reason of the segregation complained of, deprived of the equal protection of the laws guaranteed by the Fourteenth Amendment. This disposition makes unnecessary any discussion whether such segregation also violates the Due Process Clause of the Fourteenth Amendment. * * * *"

This decision was followed on May 31, 1955 by *Brown* v. *Board of Education,* 349 U.S. 294:

Mr. Chief Justice Warren delivered the opinion of the Court.

These cases were decided on May 17, 1954. The opinions of that date, declaring the fundamental principle that racial discrimination in public education is unconstitutional, are incorporated herein by reference. All provisions of federal, state, or local law requiring or permitting such discrimination must yield to this principle. There remains for consideration the manner in which relief is to be accorded.

Because these cases arose under different local conditions and their disposition will involve a variety of local problems, we requested further argument on the question of relief. In view of the nationwide importance of the decision, we invited the Attorney General of the United States and the Attorneys General of all states requiring or permitting racial discrimination in public education to present their views on that question. The parties, the United States, and the States of Florida, North Carolina, Arkansas, Oklahoma, Maryland, and Texas filed briefs and participated in the oral argument.

These presentations were informative and helpful to the Court in its consideration of the complexities arising from the transition to a system of public education freed of racial discrimination. The presentations also demonstrated that substantial steps to eliminate racial discrimination in public schools have already been taken, not only in some of the communities in which these cases arose, but in some of the states appearing as *amici curiae,* and in other states as well. Substantial progress has been made in the District of Columbia and in the communities in Kansas and Delaware involved in this litigation. The defendants in the cases coming to us from South Carolina and Virginia are awaiting the decision of this Court concerning relief.

Full implementation of these constitutional principles may require solution of varied local school problems. School authorities have the primary responsibility for elucidating, assessing, and solving these problems; courts will have to consider whether the action of school authorities constitutes good faith implementation of the governing constitutional principles. Because of their proximity to local conditions and the possible need for further hearings, the courts which orginally heard these cases can best perform this judicial appraisal. Accordingly, we believe it appropriate to remand the cases to those courts.

In fashioning and effectuating the decrees, the courts will be guided by equitable principles. Traditionally, equity has been characterized by a practical flexibility in shaping its remedies and by a facility for adjusting and reconciling public and private needs. These cases call for the exercise of these traditional attributes of equity power. At stake is the personal interest of the plaintiffs in admission to public schools as soon as practicable on a nondiscriminatory basis. To effectuate this interest may call for elimination of a variety of obstacles in making the transition to school systems operated in accordance with the constitutional principles set forth in our May 17, 1954, decision. Courts of equity may properly take into account the public interest in the elimination of such obstacles in a systematic and effective manner. But it should go without saying that the vitality of these constitutional principles cannot be allowed to yield simply because of disagreement with them.

While giving weight to these public and private considerations, the courts will require that the defendants make a prompt and reasonable start toward full compliance with our May 17, 1954, ruling. Once such a start has been made, the courts may find that additional time is necessary to carry out the ruling in an effective manner. The burden rests upon the defendants to establish that such time is necessary in the public interest and is consistent with good faith compliance at the earliest practicable date. To that end, the courts may consider problems related to administration, arising from the physical condition of the school plant, the school transportation system, personnel, revision of school districts and attendance areas into compact units to achieve a system of determining admission to the public schools on a nonracial basis, and revision of local laws and regulations which may be necessary in solving the foregoing problems. They will also consider the adequacy of any plans the defendants may propose to meet these problems and to effectuate a transition to a racially nondiscriminatory school system. During this period of transition, the courts will retain jurisdiction of these cases.

The judgments below, except that in the Delaware case, are accordingly reversed and the cases are remanded to the District Courts to take such proceedings and enter such orders and decrees consistent with this opinion as are necessary and proper to admit to public schools on a racially nondiscriminatory basis with all deliberate speed the parties to these cases. The judgment in the Delaware case—ordering the immediate admission of the plaintiffs to schools previously attended only by white children—is affirmed on the basis of the principles stated in our May 17, 1954, opinion, but the case is remanded to the Supreme Court of Delaware for such further proceedings as that Court may deem necessary in light of this opinion.

It is so ordered.

# President Kennedy's message to Congress

FEBRUARY 28, 1963

"OUR CONSTITUTION is color blind," wrote Mr. Justice Harlan before the turn of the century, "and neither knows nor tolerates classes among citizens." But the practices of the country do not always conform to the principles of the Constitution. And this message is intended to examine how far we have come in achieving first-class citizenship for all citizens regardless of color, how far we have yet to go, and what further tasks remain to be carried out—by the Executive and Legislative Branches of the Federal Government, as well as by state and local governments and private citizens and organizations.

One hundred years ago the Emancipation Proclamation was signed by a President who believed in the equal worth and opportunity of every human being. That Proclamation was only a first step—a step which its author unhappily did not live to follow up, a step which some of its critics dismissed as an action which "frees the slave but ignores the Negro." Through these long one hundred years, while slavery has vanished, progress for the Negro has been too often blocked and delayed. Equality before the law has not always meant equal treatment and opportunity. And the harmful, wasteful and wrongful results of racial discrimination and segregation still appear in virtually every aspect of national life, in virtually every part of the Nation.

The Negro baby born in America today—regardless of the section or state in which he is born—has about one half as much chance of completing high school as a white baby born in the same place on the same day —one third as much chance of completing college—one third as much chance of becoming a professional man— twice as much chance of becoming unemployed—about one seventh as much chance of earning $10,000 per year —life expectancy which is seven years less—and the prospects of earning only half as much.

No American who believes in the basic truth that "all men are created equal, that they are endowed by their Creator with certain unalienable rights," can fully excuse, explain or defend the picture these statistics portray. Race discrimination hampers our economic growth by preventing the maximum development and utilization of our manpower. It hampers our world leadership by contradicting at home the message we preach abroad. It mars the atmosphere of a united and classless society in which this Nation rose to greatness. It increases the costs of public welfare, crime, delinquency and disorder. Above all, it is wrong.

Therefore, let it be clear, in our own hearts and minds, that it is not merely because of the cold war, and not merely because of the economic waste of discrimination, that we are committed to achieving true equality of opportunity. The basic reason is because it is right.

The cruel disease of discrimination knows no sectional or state boundaries. The continuing attack on this problem must be equally broad. It must be both private and public—it must be conducted at national, state and local levels—and it must include both legislative and executive action.

In the last two years, more progress has been made in securing the civil rights of all Americans than in any comparable period in our history. Progress has been made—through executive action, litigation, persuasion and private initiative—in achieving and protecting equality of opportunity in education, voting, transportation, employment, housing, government, and the enjoyment of public accommodations.

But pride in our progress must not give way to relaxation of our effort. Nor does progress in the Executive Branch enable the Legislative Branch to escape its own obligations. On the contrary, it is in the light of this Nation-wide progress, and in the belief that Congress will wish once again to meet its responsibilities in this matter, that I stress in the following agenda of existing and prospective action important legislative as well as administrative measures.

## I. THE RIGHT TO VOTE

The right to vote in a free American election is the most powerful and precious right in the world—and it must not be denied on the grounds of race or color. It is a potent key to achieving other rights of citizenship. For American history—both recent and past—clearly reveals that the power of the ballot has enabled those who achieve it to win other achievements as well, to gain a full voice in the affairs of their state and nation, and to see their interests represented in the governmental bodies which affect their future. In a free society, those with the power to govern are necessarily responsive to those with the right to vote.

In enacting the 1957 and 1960 Civil Rights Acts, Congress provided the Department of Justice with basic tools for protecting the right to vote—and this Administration has not hesitated to use those tools. Legal action is brought only after voluntary efforts fail—and, in scores of instances, local officials, at the request of the Department of Justice, have voluntarily made voting records available or abandoned discriminatory registration, discriminatory voting practices or segregated balloting. Where voluntary local compliance has not been forthcoming, the Department of Justice has approximately quadrupled the previous level of its legal effort —investigating coercion, inspecting records, initiating lawsuits, enjoying intimidation, and taking whatever follow-up action is necessary to forbid further interference or discrimination. As a result, thousands of Negro citizens are registering and voting for the first time—many of them in counties where no Negro had ever voted before. *The Department of Justice will continue to take whatever action is required to secure the right to vote for all Americans.*

Experience has shown, however, that these highly useful Acts of the 85th and 86th Congresses suffer from two major defects. One is the usual long and difficult delay which occurs between the filing of a lawsuit and its ultimate conclusion. In one recent case, for example, nineteen months elapsed between the filing of the suit and the judgment of the court. In another, an action brought in July, 1961, has not yet come to trial. The legal maxim "Justice delayed is Justice denied" is dramatically applicable in these cases.

Too often those who attempt to assert their constitutional rights are intimidated. Prospective registrants are fired. Registration workers are arrested. In some instances, churches in which registration meetings are held have been burned. In one case where Negro tenant farmers chose to exercise their right to vote, it was necessary for the Justice Department to seek injunctions to halt their eviction and for the Department of Agriculture to help feed them from surplus stocks. Under these circumstances, continued delay in the granting of the franchise—particularly in counties where there is mass racial disfranchisement—permits the intent of the Congress to be openly flouted.

Federal executive action in such cases—no matter how speedy and how drastic—can never fully correct such abuses of power. It is necessary instead to free the forces of our democratic system within these areas by promptly insuring the franchise to all citizens, making it possible for their elected officials to be truly responsive to all their constituents.

The second and somewhat overlapping gap in these statutes is their failure to deal specifically with the most common forms of abuse of discretion on the part of local election officials who do not treat all applicants uniformly.

Objections were raised last year to the proposed literacy test bill, which attempts to speed up the enforcement of the right to vote by removing one important area of discretion from registration officials who used that discretion to exclude Negroes. Preventing that bill from coming to a vote did not make any less real the prevalence in many counties of the use of literacy and other voter qualification tests to discriminate against prospective Negro voters, contrary to the requirements of the 14th and 15th Amendments, and adding to the delays and difficulties encountered in securing the franchise for those denied it.

An indication of the magnitude of the over-all problem, as well as the need for speedy action, is a recent five-state survey disclosing over 200 counties in which fewer than 15 percent of the Negroes of voting age are registered to vote. This cannot continue. I am, therefore, recommending legislation to deal with this problem of judicial delay and administrative abuse in four ways:

• *First, to provide for interim relief while voting suits are proceeding through the courts in areas of demonstrated need, temporary Federal voting referees should be appointed to determine the qualifications of applicants for registration and voting during the pendency of a lawsuit in any county in which fewer than 15 per cent of the eligible number of persons of any race claimed to be discriminated against are registered to vote.* Existing Federal law provides for the appointment of voting referees to receive and act upon applications for voting registration upon a court finding that a pattern or practice of discrimination exists. But to prevent a successful case from becoming an empty victory, insofar as the particular election is concerned, the proposed legislation would provide that, within these prescribed limits, temporary voting referees would be appointed to serve from the inception to the conclusion of the Federal voting suit, applying, however, only state law and state regulations. As officers of the court, their decisions would be subject to court scrutiny and review.

• *Second, voting suits brought under the Federal Civil Rights statutes should be accorded expedited treatment in the Federal courts,* just as in many state courts election suits are given preference on the dockets on the sensible premise that, unless the right to vote can be exercised at a specific election, it is, to the extent of that election, lost forever.

• *Third, the law should specifically prohibit the application of different tests, standards, practices or procedures for different applicants seeking to register and vote in Federal elections.* Under present law, the courts can ultimately deal with the various forms of racial discrimination practiced by local registrars. But the task of litigation, and the time consumed in preparation and proof, should be lightened in every possible fashion. No one can rightfully contend that any voting registrar should be permitted to deny the vote to any qualified citizen, anywhere in this country, through discriminatory administration of qualifying tests, or upon the basis of minor errors in filling out a complicated form which seeks only information. Yet the Civil Rights Commission, and the cases brought by the Department of Justice, have compiled one discouraging example after another of obstacles placed in the path of Negroes seeking to register to vote at the same time that other applicants experience no difficulty whatsoever. Qualified

Negroes, including those with college degrees, have been denied registration for their inability to give a "reasonable" interpretation of the Constitution. They have been required to complete their applications with unreasonable precision—or to secure registered voters to vouch for their identity—or to defer to white persons who want to register ahead of them—or they are otherwise subjected to exasperating delays. Yet uniformity of treatment is required by the dictates of both the Constitution and fair play—and this proposed statute, therefore, seeks to spell out that principle to ease the difficulties and delays of litigation. Limiting the proposal to voting qualifications in elections for Federal offices alone will clearly eliminate any constitutional conflict.

• *Fourth, completion of the sixth grade should, with respect to Federal elections, constitute a presumption that the applicant is literate.* Literacy tests pose especially difficult problems in determining voter qualification. The essentially subjective judgment involved in each individual case, and the difficulty of challenging that judgment, have made literacy tests one of the cruelest and most abused of all voter qualification tests. The incidence of such abuse can be eliminated, or at least drastically curtailed, by the proposed legislation providing that proof of completion of the sixth grade constitutes a presumption that the applicant is literate.

• Finally, the 87th Congress—after 20 years of effort —passed and referred to the states for ratification a Constitutional Amendment to prohibit the levying of poll taxes as a condition to voting. Already 13 states have ratified the proposed Amendment and in three more one body of the legislature has acted. I urge every state legislature to take prompt action on this matter and to outlaw the poll tax—which has too long been an outmoded and arbitrary bar to voting participation by minority groups and others—as the 24th Amendment to the Constitution. This measure received bi-partisan sponsorship and endorsement in the Congress—and I *shall continue to work with governors and legislative leaders of both parties in securing adoption of the anti-poll tax amendment.*

## II. EDUCATION

Nearly nine years have elapsed since the Supreme Court ruled that state laws requiring or permitting segregated schools violate the Constitution. That decision represented both good law and good judgment—it was both legally and morally right. Since that time it has become increasingly clear that neither violence nor legalistic evasions will be tolerated as a means of thwarting court-ordered desegregation, that closed schools are not an answer, and that responsible communities are able to handle the desegregation process in a calm and sensible manner. This is as it should be—for, as I stated to the Nation at the time of the Mississippi violence last September:

". . . Our Nation is founded on the principle that observance of the law is the eternal safeguard of liberty, and defiance of the law is the surest road to tyranny. The law which we obey includes the final rulings of the courts, as well as the enactments of our legislative bodies. Even among law-abiding men, few laws are universally loved—but they are uniformly respected and not resisted.

"Americans are free to disagree with the law but not to disobey it. For in a government of laws and not of men, no man, however prominent or powerful, and no mob, however unruly or boisterous, is entitled to defy a court of law. If this country should ever reach the point where any man or group of men, by force or threat of force, could long defy the commands of our court and our Constitution, then no law would stand free from doubt, no judge would be sure of his writ, and no citizen would be safe from his neighbors."

The shameful violence which accompanied but did not prevent the end of segregation at the University of Mississippi was an exception. State-supported universities in Georgia and South Carolina met this test in recent years with calm and maturity, as did the state-supported universities of Virginia, North Carolina, Florida, Texas, Louisiana, Tennessee, Arkansas and Kentucky in earlier years. In addition, progress toward the desegregation of education at all levels has made other notable and peaceful strides, including the following forward moves in the last two years alone:

• Desegregation plans have been put into effect peacefully in the public schools of Atlanta, Dallas, New Orleans, Memphis and elsewhere, with over 60 school districts desegregated last year—frequently with the help of Federal persuasion and consultation, and in every case without incident or disorder.

• Teacher training institutes financed under the National Defense Education Act are no longer held in colleges which refuse to accept students without regard to race, and this has resulted in a number of institutions opening their doors to Negro applicants voluntarily.

• The same is now true of Institutes conducted by the National Science Foundation.

• Beginning in September of this year, under the Aid to Impacted Area School Program, the Department of Health, Education, and Welfare will initiate a program of providing on-base facilities so that children living on military installations will no longer be required to attend segregated schools at Federal expense. These children should not be victimized by segregation merely because their fathers chose to serve in the armed forces and were assigned to an area where schools are operated on a segregated basis.

• In addition, the Department of Justice and the Department of Health, Education and Welfare have succeeded in obtaining voluntary desegregation in many other districts receiving "impacted area" school assistance; and representing the Federal interest, have filed lawsuits to end segregation in a number of other districts.

• The Department of Justice has also intervened to seek the opening of public schools in the case of Prince Edward County, Virginia, the only county in the Nation where there are no public schools, and where a bitter effort to thwart court decrees requiring desegregation has caused nearly 1500 out of 1800 school age Negro children to go without any education for more than 3 years.

*In these and other areas within its jurisdiction, the Executive Branch will continue its efforts to fulfill the constitutional objective of an equal, non-segregated, educational opportunity for all children.*

Despite these efforts, however, progress toward primary and secondary school desegregation has still been too slow, often painfully so. Those children who are being denied their constitutional rights are suffering a loss which can never be regained, and which will leave scars which can never be fully healed. I have in the past expressed my belief that the full authority of the Federal Government should be placed behind the achievement of school desegregation, in accordance with the command of the Constitution. One obvious area of Federal action is to help facilitate the transition to desegregation in those areas which are conforming or wish to conform their practices to the law.

Many of these communities lack the resources necessary to eliminate segregation in their public schools while at the same time assuring that educational standards will be maintained and improved. The problem has been compounded by the fact that the climate of mistrust in many communities has left many school officials with no qualified source to turn to for information and advice.

There is a need for technical assistance by the Office of Education to assist local communities in preparing and carrying out desegregation plans, including the supplying of information on means which have been employed to desegregate other schols successfully. There is also need for financial assistance to enable those communities which desire and need such assistance to employ specialized personnel to cope with problems occasioned by desegregation and to train school personnel to facilitate the transition to desegregation. While some facilities for providing this kind of assistance are presently available in the Office of Education, they are not adequate to the task.

*I recommend, therefore, a program of Federal technical and financial assistance to aid school districts in the process of desegregation in compliance with the Constitution.*

Finally, it is obvious that the unconstitutional and outmoded concept of "separate but equal" does not belong in the Federal statute books. This is particularly true with respect to higher education, where peaceful desegregation has been under way in practically every state for some time. *I repeat, therefore, this Administration's recommendation of last year that this phrase be eliminated from the Morrill Land Grant College Act.*

### III. EXTENSION AND EXPANSION OF THE COMMISSION ON CIVIL RIGHTS

The Commission on Civil Rights established by the Civil Rights Act of 1957, has been in operation for more than five years and is scheduled to expire on Nov. 30, 1963. During this time it has fulfilled its statutory mandate by investigating deprivations of the right to vote and denials of equal protection of the laws in education, employment, housing and the administration of justice. The Commission's reports and recommendations have provided the basis for remedial action both by Congress and the Executive Branch.

There are, of course, many areas of denials of rights yet to be fully investigated. But the Commission is now in a position to provide even more useful service to the Nation. As more communities evidence a willingness to face frankly their problems of racial discrimination, there is an increasing need for expert guidance and assistance in devising workable programs for civil rights progress. Agencies of state and local government, industry, labor and community organizations, when faced with problems of segregation and racial tensions, all can benefit from information about how these problems have been solved in the past.

The opportunity to seek an experienced and sympathetic forum on a voluntary basis can often open channels of communication between contending parties and help bring about the conditions necessary for orderly progress. And the use of public hearings—to contribute to public knowledge of the requirements of the Constitution and national policy—can create in these communities the atmosphere of understanding which is indispensable to peaceful and permanent solutions to racial problems.

The Federal Civil Rights Commission has the experience and capability to make a significant contribution toward achieving these objectives. It has advised the Executive Branch not only about desirable policy changes but about the adminstrative techniques needed to make these changes effective. If, however, the Commission is to perform these additional services effectively, changes in its authorizing statute are necessary and it should be placed on a more stable and more permanent basis. A proposal that the Commission be made a permanent body would be a pessimistic prediction that our problems will never be solved. On the other hand, to let the experience and knowledge gathered by the Commission go to waste, by allowing it to expire, or by extending its life only for another two years with no change in responsibility, would ignore the very real contribution this agency can make toward meeting our racial problems.

*I recommend, therefore, that the Congress authorize the Civil Rights Commission to serve as a national civil rights clearing house providing information, advice, and technical assistance to any requesting agency, private or public; that in order to fulfill these new responsibilities, the Commission be authorized to concentrate its activities upon those problems within the scope of its statute which most need attention; and that the life of the Commission be extended for a term of at least four more years.*

## IV. EMPLOYMENT

Racial discrimination in employment is especially injurious both to its victims and to the national economy. It results in a great waste of human resources and creates serious community problems. It is, moreover, inconsistent with the democratic principle that no man should be denied employment commensurate with his abilities because of his race or creed or ancestry.

The President's Committee on Equal Employment Opportunity, reconstituted by Executive Order in early 1961, has, under the leadership of the Vice President, taken significant steps to eliminate racial discrimination by those who do business with the Government. Hundreds of companies—covering 17 million jobs—have agreed to stringent nondiscriminatory provisions now standard in all Government contracts. One hundred four industrial concerns—including most of the Nation's major employers—have in addition signed agreements calling for an affirmative attack on discrimination in employment; and 117 labor unions, representing about 85% of the membership of the AFL-CIO, have signed similar agreements with the Committee.

Comprehensive compliance machinery has been instituted to enforce these agreements. The Committee has received over 1,300 complaints in two years—more than in the entire 7½ years of the Committee's prior existence—and has achieved corrective action on 72% of the cases handled—a heartening and unprecedented record. Significant results have been achieved in placing Negroes with contractors who previously employed whites only—and in the elevation of Negroes to a far higher proportion of professional, technical and supervisory jobs. *Let me repeat my assurances that these provisions in Government contracts and the voluntary nondiscrimination agreements will be carefully monitored and strictly enforced.*

In addition, the Federal Government, as an employer, has continued to pursue a policy of nondiscrimination in its employment and promotion programs. Negro high-school and college graduates are now being intensively sought out and recruited. A policy of not distinguishing on grounds of race is not limited to the appointment of distinguished Negroes—although they have in fact been appointed to a record number of high policy-making, judicial and administrative posts. There has also been a significant increase in the number of Negroes employed in the middle and upper grades of the career Federal service. In jobs paying $4,500 to $10,000 annually, for example, there was an increase of 20% in the number of Negroes during the year ending June 30, 1962—over three times the rate of increase for all employes in those grades during the year. *Career civil servants will continue to be employed and promoted on the basis of merit, and not color, in every agency of the Federal Government, including all regional and local offices.*

This Government has also adopted a new Executive policy with respect to the organization of its employes. As part of this policy, only *those Federal employe labor organizations that do not discriminate on grounds of race or color will be recognized.*

Outside of Government employment, the National Labor Relations Board is now considering cases involving charges of racial discrimination against a number of union locals. *I have directed the Department of Justice to participate in these cases and to urge the National Labor Relations Board to take appropriate action against racial discrimination in unions.* It is my hope that administrative action and litigation will make unnecessary the enactment of legislation with respect to union discrimination.

### V. PUBLIC ACCOMMODATIONS

No act is more contrary to the spirit of our democracy and Constitution—or more rightfully resented by a Negro citizen who seeks only equal treatment—than the barring of that citizen from restaurants, hotels, theaters, recreational areas and other public accommodations and facilities.

Wherever possible, this Administration has dealt sternly with such acts. In 1961, the Justice Department and the Interstate Commerce Commission successfully took action to bring an end to discrimination in rail and bus facilities. In 1962, the 15 airports still maintaining segregated facilities were persuaded to change their practices, 13 voluntarily and two others after the Department of Justice brought legal action. As a result of these steps, systematic segregation in interstate transportation has virtually ceased to exist. No doubt isolated instances of discrimination in transportation terminals, restaurants, rest rooms and other facilities will continue to crop up, but *any such discrimination will be dealt with promptly.*

In addition, restaurants and public facilities in buildings leased by the Federal Government have been opened up to all Federal employes in areas where previously they had been segregated. The General Services Administration no longer contracts for the lease of space in office buildings unless such facilities are available to all Federal employes without regard to race. This move has taken place without fanfare and practically without incident; *and full equality of facilities will continue to be made available to all Federal employes in every state.*

National parks, forests and other recreation areas— and the District of Columbia Stadium—are open to all without regard to race. Meetings sponsored by the Federal Government or addressed by Federal appointees are held in hotels and halls which do not practice discrimination or segregation. The Department of Justice has asked the Supreme Court to reverse the convictions of Negroes arrested for seeking to use public accommodations; and took action both through the courts and the use of Federal marshals to protect those who were testing the desegregation of transportation facilities.

In these and other ways, the Federal Government will continue to encourage and support action by state and local communities, and by private entrepreneurs, to assure all members of the public equal access to all public accommodations. A country with a "color blind" Constitution, and with no castes or classes among its citizens, cannot afford to do less.

### VI. OTHER USES OF FEDERAL FUNDS

The basic standard of non-discrimination—which I earlier stated has now been applied by the Executive Branch to every area of its activity—affects other programs not listed above:

• Although President Truman ordered the armed services of this country desegregated in 1948, it was necessary in 1962 to bar segregation formally and specifically in the Army and Air Force Reserves and in the training of all civil defense workers.

• A new Executive Order on housing, as unanimously recommended by the Civil Rights Commission in 1959, prohibits discrimination in the sale, lease or use of housing owned or constructed in the future by the Federal

Government or guaranteed under the FHA, VA and Farmers Home Administration program. With regard to existing property owned or financed through the Federal Government, the departments and agencies are directed to take every appropriate action to promote the termination of discriminatory practices that may exist. A President's Committee on Equal Housing Opportunity was created by the Order to implement its provisions.

• A Committee on Equal Opportunity in the Armed Forces has been established to investigate and make recommendations regarding the treatment of minority groups, with special emphasis on off-base problems.

• The U.S. Coast Guard Academy now has Negro students for the first time in its 87 years of existence.

• The Department of Justice has increased its prosecution of police brutality cases, many of them in Northern states—and is assisting state and local departments in meeting this problem.

• State employe merit systems operating programs financed with Federal funds are now prohibited from discriminating on the basis of race or color.

• The Justice Department is challenging the constitutionality of the "separate but equal" provisions which permit hospitals constructed with Federal funds to discriminate racially in the location of patients and the acceptance of doctors.

In short, the Executive Branch of the Federal Government, under this Administration and in all of its activities, now stands squarely behind the principle of equal opportunity, without segregation or discrimination, in the employment of Federal funds, facilities and personnel. All officials at every level are charged with the responsibility of implementing this principle—and a formal interdepartmental action group, under White House chairmanship, oversees this effort and follows through on each directive. For the first time, the full force of Federal executive authority is being exerted in the battle against race discrimination.

## CONCLUSION

The various steps which have been undertaken or which are proposed in this message do not constitute a final answer to the problems of race discrimination in this country. They do constitute a list of priorities— steps which can be taken by the Executive Branch and measures which can be enacted by the 88th Congress. Other measures directed toward these same goals will be favorably commented on and supported, as they have in the past—and they will be signed, if enacted into law.

In addition, it is my hope that this message will lend encouragement to those state and local governments— and to private organizations, corporations and individuals—who share my concern over the gap between our precepts and our practices. This is an effort in which every individual who asks what he can do for his country should be able and willing to take part. It is important, for example, for private citizens and local governments to support the State Department's efforts to end the discriminatory treatment suffered by too many foreign diplomats, students and visitors to this country. But it is not enough to treat those from other lands with equality and dignity—the same treatment must be afforded to every American citizen.

The program outlined in this message should not provide the occasion for sectional bitterness. No state or section of this Nation can pretend a self-righteous role, for every area has its own civil rights problems.

Nor should the basic elements of this program be imperiled by partisanship. The proposals put forth are consistent with the platforms of both parties and with the positions of their leaders. Inevitably there will be disagreement about means and strategy. But I would hope that on issues of constitutional rights and freedom, as in matters affecting our national security, there is a fundamental unity among us that will survive partisan debate over particular issues.

The centennial of the issuance of the Emancipation Proclamation is an occasion for celebration, for a sober assessment of our failures, and for rededication to the goals of freedom. Surely there could be no more meaningful observance of the centennial than the enactment of effective civil rights legislation and the continuation of effective executive action.

# "*A section reserved for whites*"

FORD T. JOHNSON, JR., V. VIRGINIA

ON PETITION FOR WRIT OF CERTIORARI TO
THE SUPREME COURT OF APPEALS OF VIRGINIA

NO. 715.    DECIDED APRIL 29, 1963

―――

PER CURIAM.

The petition for a writ of certiorari is granted, the judgment of the Supreme Court of Appeals of Virginia is reversed, and the case is remanded for proceedings not inconsistent with this opinion.

The petitioner, Ford T. Johnson, was convicted of contempt of the Traffic Court of the City of Richmond, Virginia, and appealed his conviction to the Hustings Court, where he was tried without a jury and again convicted. The Supreme Court of Appeals of Virginia refused to grant a writ of error on the ground that the judgment appealed from was "plainly right," but the Chief Justice of that court stayed execution of the judgment pending disposition of this petition for certiorari.

The evidence at petitioner's trial in the Hustings Court is summarized in an approved statement of facts. According to this statement, the witnesses for the State testified as follows: The petitioner, a Negro, was seated in the Traffic Court in a section reserved for whites, and when requested to move by the bailiff, refused to do so.

The judge then summoned the petitioner to the bench and instructed him to be seated in the right hand section of the courtroom, the section reserved for Negroes. The petitioner moved back in front of the counsel table and remained standing with his arms folded, stating that he preferred standing and indicating that he would not comply with the judge's order. Upon refusal to obey the judge's further direction to be seated, the petitioner was arrested for contempt. At no time did he behave in a boisterous or abusive manner, and there was no disorder in the courtroom. The State, in its Brief in Opposition filed in this Court, concedes that in the section of the Richmond Traffic Court reserved for spectators, seating space "is assigned on the basis of racial designation, the seats on one side of the aisle being for use of Negro citizens and the seats on the other side being for use of white citizens."

It is clear from the totality of circumstances, and particularly the fact that the petitioner was peaceably seated in the section reserved for whites before being summoned to the bench, that the arrest and conviction rested entirely on the refusal to comply with the segregated seating requirements imposed in this particular courtroom. Such a conviction cannot stand, for it is no longer open to question that a State may not constitutionally require segregation of public facilities. See, *e.g.*, *Brown* v. *Board of Education*, 347 U.S. 483; *Mayor and City Council of Baltimore* v. *Dawson*, 350 U.S. 877; *Turner* v. *Memphis*, 369 U.S. 350. State-compelled segregation in a court of justice is a manifest violation of the State's duty to deny no one the equal protection of its laws.

*Reversed and remanded*

# "Unlawful to furnish meals to white persons and colored persons at same counter"

JAMES RICHARD PETERSON V. CITY OF GREENVILLE

DECIDED MAY 20, 1963

MR. CHIEF JUSTICE WARREN delivered the opinion of the Court.

The petitioners were convicted in the Recorder's Court of the City of Greenville, South Carolina, for violating the trespass statute of that State. Each was sentenced to pay a fine of $100 or in lieu thereof to serve 30 days in jail. * * *

The 10 petitioners are Negro boys and girls who, on August 9, 1960, entered the S. H. Kress store in Greenville and seated themselves at the lunch counter for the purpose, as they testified, of being served. When the Kress manager observed the petitioners sitting at the counter, he "had one of [his] . . . employees call the Police Department and turn off the lights and state the lunch counter was closed." A captain of police and two other officers responded by proceeding to the store in a patrol car where they were met by other policemen and two state agents who had preceded them there. In the presence of the police and the state agents, the manager "announced that the lunch counter was being closed and would everyone leave" the area. The petitioners, who had been sitting at the counter for five minutes, remained seated and were promptly arrested. The boys were searched, and both boys and girls were taken to police headquarters.

The manager of the store did not request the police to arrest petitioners; he asked them to leave because integrated service was "contrary to local customs" of segregation at lunch counters and in violation of the following Greenville City ordinance requiring separation of the races in restaurants:

"It shall be unlawful for any person owning, managing or controlling any hotel, restaurant, cafe, eating house, boarding house or similar establishment to furnish meals to white persons and colored persons in the same room, or at the same table, or at the same counter; provided, however, that meals may be served to white persons and colored persons in the same room where separate facilities are furnished. Separate facilities shall be interpreted to mean:

"(a) Separate eating utensils and separate dishes for the serving of food, all of which shall be distinctly marked by some appropriate color scheme or otherwise;

"(b) Separate tables, counters or booths;

"(c) A distance of at least thirty-five feet shall be maintained between the area where white and colored persons are served;

"(d) The area referred to in subsection (c) above

shall not be vacant but shall be occupied by the usual display counters and merchandise found in a business concern of a similar nature;

"(e) A separate facility shall be maintained and used for the cleaning of eating utensils and dishes furnished the two races." Code of Greenville, 1953, as amended in 1958, §31–8.

The manager and the police conceded that the petitioners were clean, well dressed, unoffensive in conduct, and that they sat quietly at the counter which was designed to accommodate 59 persons. The manager described his establishment as a national chain store of 15 or 20 departments, selling over 10,000 items. He stated that the general public was invited to do business at the store and that the patronage of Negroes was solicited in all departments of the store other than the lunch counter.

Petitioners maintain that South Carolina has denied them rights of free speech, both because their activity was protected by the First and Fourteenth Amendments and because the trespass statute did not require a showing that the Kress manager gave them notice of his authority when he asked them to leave. Petitioners also assert that they have been deprived of the equal protection of the laws secured to them against state action by the Fourteenth Amendment. We need decide only the last of the questions thus raised.

The evidence in this case establishes beyond doubt that the Kress management's decision to exclude petitioners from the lunch counter was made because they were Negroes. It cannot be disputed that under our decisions "Private conduct abridging individual rights does no violence to the Equal Protection Clause unless to some significant extent the state in any of its manifestations has been found to have become involved in it." *Burton* v. *Wilmington Parking Authority,* 365 U.S. 715, 722; *Turner* v. *City of Memphis,* 369 U.S. 350.

It cannot be denied that here the City of Greenville, an agency of the State, has provided by its ordinance that the decision as to whether a restaurant facility is to be operated on a desegregated basis is to be reserved to it. When the State has commanded a particular result it has saved to itself the power to determine that result and thereby "to a significant extent" has "become involved" in, and in fact, has removed that decision from the sphere of private choice. It has thus effectively determined that a person owning, managing or controlling an eating place is left with no choice of his own but must segregate his white and Negro patrons. The Kress management, in deciding to exclude Negroes, did precisely what the city law required.

Consequently these convictions cannot stand, even assuming, as respondent contends, that the manager would have acted as he did independently of the existence of the ordinance. The State will not be heard to make this contention in support of the convictions. For the convictions had the effect, which the State cannot deny, of enforcing the ordinance passed by the City of Greenville, the agency of the State. When a state agency passes a law compelling persons to discriminate against other persons because of race, and the State's criminal processes are employed in a way which enforces the discrimination mandated by that law, such a palpable violation of the Fourteenth Amendment cannot be saved by attempting to separate the mental urges of the discriminators.

*Reversed.*

MR. JUSTICE HARLAN concurred in the result in a separate opinion.

# "I am not allowed to serve you here"

## RUDOLPH LOMBARD V. STATE OF LOUISIANA
### DECIDED MAY 20, 1963

=====

MR. CHIEF JUSTICE WARREN delivered the opinion of the Court.

This case presents for review trespass convictions resulting from an attempt by Negroes to be served in a privately owned restaurant customarily patronized only by whites. However, unlike a number of the cases this day decided, no state statute or city ordinance here forbids desegregation of the races in all restaurant facilities. Nevertheless, we conclude that this case is governed by the principles announced in *Peterson* v. *City of Greenville,* * * * and that the convictions for this reason must be reversed.

Petitioners are three Negroes and one white, college students. On September 17, 1960, at about 10:30 in the morning they entered the McCrory Five and Ten Cent Store in New Orleans, Louisiana. They sat down at a refreshment counter at the back of the store and requested service which was refused. Although no sign so indicated, the management operated the counter on a segregated basis, serving only white patrons. The counter was designed to accommodate 24 persons. Negroes were

*219*

welcome to shop in other areas of the store. The restaurant manager, believing that the "unusual circumstance" of Negroes sitting at the counter created an "emergency," asked petitioners to leave and, when they did not do so, ordered that the counter be closed. The restaurant manager then contacted the store manager and called the police. He frankly testified that the petitioners did not cause any disturbance, that they were orderly, and that he asked them to leave because they were Negroes. Presumably he asked the white petitioner to leave because he was in the company of Negroes.

A number of police officers, including a captain and major of police, arrived at the store shortly after they were called. Three of the officers had a conference with the store manager. The store manager then went behind the counter, faced petitioners, and in a loud voice asked them to leave. He also testified that the petitioners were merely sitting quietly at the counter throughout these happenings. When petitioners remained seated, the police major spoke to petitioner Goldfinch, and asked him what they were doing there. Mr. Goldfinch replied that petitioners "were going to sit there until they were going to be served." When petitioners still declined to leave, they were arrested by the police, led out of the store, and taken away in a patrol wagon. They were later tried and convicted for violation of the Louisiana criminal mischief statute. This statute, in its application to this case, has all the elements of the usual trespass statute. Each petitioner was sentenced to serve 60 days in the Parish Prison and to pay a fine of $350. In default of payment of the fine each is to serve 60 additional days in prison. * * *

Prior to this occurrence New Orleans city officials, characterizing conduct such as petitioners were arrested for as "sit-in demonstrations," had determined that such attempts to secure desegregated service, though orderly and possibly inoffensive to local merchants, would not be permitted.

Exactly one week earlier, on September 10, 1960, a like occurrence had taken place in a Woolworth store in the same city. In immediate reaction thereto the Superintendent of Police issued a highly publicized statement which discussed the incident and stated that "We wish to urge the parents of both white and Negro students who participated in today's sit-in demonstration to urge upon these young people that such actions are not in the community interest. . . . [W]e want everyone to fully understand that the police department and its personnel is ready and able to enforce the laws of the city of New Orleans and the state of Louisiana." On September 13, four days before petitioners' arrest, the Mayor of New Orleans issued an unequivocal statement condemning such conduct and demanding its cessation. This statement was also widely publicized; it read in part:

"I have today directed the Superintendent of Police that no additional sit-in demonstrations . . . will be permitted . . . regardless of the avowed purpose or intent of the participants. . . .

.   .   .   .   .   .

"It is my determination that the community interest, the public safety, and the economic welfare of this city require that such demonstrations cease and that henceforth they be prohibited by the police department."

Both statements were publicized in the New Orleans Times-Picayune. The Mayor and the Superintendent of Police both testified that, to their knowledge, no eating establishment in New Orleans operated desegregated eating facilities.

Both the restaurant manager and the store manager asked the petitioners to leave. Petitioners were charged with failing to leave at the request of the store manager. There was evidence to indicate that the restaurant manager asked petitioners to leave in obedience to the directive of the city officials. He told them that "I am not allowed to serve you here. . . . We *have* to sell to you at the rear of the store where we have a colored counter." (Emphasis supplied.) And he called the police "[a]s a matter of routine procedure." The petitioners testified that when they did not leave, the restaurant manager whistled and the employees removed the stools, turned off the lights, and put up a sign saying that the counter was closed. One petitioner stated that "it appeared to be a very efficient thing, everyone knew what to do." The store manager conceded that his decision to operate a segregated facility "conform[ed] to state policy and practice" as well as local custom. When asked whether "in the last 30 days to 60 days [he had] entered into any conference with other department store managers here in New Orleans relative to sit-in problems," the store manager stated: "[w]e have spoken of it." The above evidence all tended to indicate that the store officials' actions were coerced by the city. But the evidence of coercion was not fully developed because the trial judge forbade petitioners to ask questions directed to that very issue.

But we need not pursue this inquiry further. A State, or a city, may act as authoritatively through its executive as through its legislative body. See *Ex parte Virginia,* 100 U.S. 339, 347. As we interpret the New Orleans city officials' statements, they here determined that the city would not permit Negroes to seek desegregated service in restaurants. Consequently, the city must be treated exactly as if it had an ordinance prohibiting such conduct. We have just held in *Peterson* v. *City of Greenville, ante, . . .* that where an ordinance makes it unlawful for owners or managers of restaurants to seat whites and Negroes together, a conviction under the State's criminal processes employed in a way which enforces the discrimination mandated by that ordinance cannot stand. Equally the State cannot achieve the same result by an official command which has at least as much coercive effect as an ordinance. The official command here was to direct continuance of segregated service in restaurants, and to prohibit any conduct directed toward its discontinuance; it was not restricted solely to preserve the public peace in a nondiscriminatory fashion in a situation where violence was present or imminent by reason of public demonstrations. Therefore here, as in *Peterson,* these convictions, commanded as they were by the voice of the State directing segregated service at the restaurant, cannot stand. *Turner* v. *City of Memphis,* 369 U.S. 350.

*Reversed.*

MR. JUSTICE HARLAN dissented in a separate opinion.

MR. JUSTICE DOUGLAS, concurring.

While I join the opinion of the Court, I have concluded it necessary to state with more particularity why Louisiana has become involved to a "significant extent" (*Burton* v. *Wilmington Parking Authority,* 365 U.S. 715, 722) in denying equal protection of the laws to petitioners.

I

The court below based its affirmance of these convictions on the ground that the decision to segregate this restaurant was a private choice, uninfluenced by the officers of the State. *State* v. *Goldfinch,* 241 La. 958, 132 So. 2d 860. If this were an intrusion of a man's home or yard or farm or garden, the property owner could seek and obtain the aid of the State against the intruder. For the Bill of Rights, as applied to the States through the Due Process Clause of the Fourteenth Amendment, casts its weight on the side of the privacy of homes. The Third Amendment with its ban on the quartering of soldiers in private homes radiates that philosophy. The Fourth Amendment, while concerned with official invasions of privacy through searches and seizures, is eloquent testimony of the sanctity of private premises. For even when the police enter private precincts they must, with rare exceptions, come armed with a warrant issued by a magistrate. A private person has no standing to obtain even limited access. The principle that a man's home is his castle is basic to our system of jurisprudence.

But a restaurant, like the other departments of this retail store where Negroes were served, though private property within the protection of the Fifth Amendment, has no aura of constitutionally protected privacy about it. Access by the public is the very reason for its existence.

"Ownership does not always mean absolute dominion. The more an owner, for his advantage, opens up his property for use by the public in general, the more do his rights become circumscribed by the statutory and constitutional rights of those who use it." *Marsh* v. *Alabama,* 326 U.S. 501, 506.

The line between a private business and a public one has been long and hotly contested. *New State Ice Co.* v. *Liebmann,* 285 U.S. 262, is one of the latest cases in a long chain. The Court, over the dissent of Mr. Justice Brandeis and Mr. Justice Stone, held unconstitutional an Oklahoma statute requiring those manufacturing ice for sale and distribution to obtain a license from the State. Mr. Justice Brandeis' dissent was in the tradition of an ancient doctrine perhaps best illustrated by *German Alliance Ins. Co.* v. *Kansas,* 233 U.S. 389, which upheld a Kansas statute that regulated fire insurance rates. Mr. Justice McKenna, writing for the Court, said, "It is the business that is the fundamental thing; property is but its instrument, the means of rendering the service which has become a public interest." *Id.,* 408. Cf. *Ferguson* v. *Skrupa,* 372 U.S. 726.

Some of the cases reflect creative attempts by judges to make innkeepers, common carriers, and the like perform the public function of taking care of all travelers. Others involve the power of the legislature to impose various kinds of restraints or conditions on business. As a result of the conjunction of various forces, judicial and legislative, it came to pass that "A large province of industrial activity is under the joint control of the market and the state."

The present case would be on all fours with the earlier ones holding that a business may be regulated when it renders a service which "has become a public interest" (*German Alliance Ins. Co.* v. *Kansas, supra,* 408) if Louisiana had declared, as do some States, that a business may not refuse service to a customer on account of race and the proprietor of the restaurant were charged with violating this statute. We should not await legislative action before declaring that state courts cannot enforce this type of segregation. Common-law judges fashioned the rules governing innkeepers and carriers. As stated by Holt, C. J., in *Lane* v. *Cotton,* 12 Mod. 472, 484 (1701):

> "[W]herever any Subject takes upon himself a Publick Trust for the Benefit of the rest of his fellow Subjects, he is *eo ipso* bound to serve the Subject in all the Things that are within the Reach and Comprehension of such an Office, under Pain of an Action against him. . . . If on the road a Shoe fall off my Horse, and I come to a Smith to have one put on, and the Smith refuse to do it, an Action will lie against him, because he has made Profession of a Trade which is for the Publick Good, and has thereby exposed and vested an interest of himself in all the King's Subjects that will employ him in the Way of his Trade. If an Inn-keeper refuse to entertain a Guest, when his House is not full, an Action will lie against him; and so against a Carrier, if his Horses be not loaded, and he refuse to take a Packet proper to be sent by a Carrier."

226

Judges who fashioned those rules had no written constitution as a guide. There were, to be sure, criminal
statutes that regulated the common callings. But the
civil remedies were judge-made. We live under a constitution that proclaims equal protection of the laws. That
standard is our guide. See *Griffin* v. *Illinois,* 351 U.S. 12;
*Douglas* v. *California,* 372 U.S. 353. And under that
standard business serving the public cannot seek the aid
of the state police or the state courts or the state legislatures to foist racial segregation in public places under its
ownership and control. The constitutional protection
extends only to "state" action, not to personal action.
But we have "state" action here, wholly apart from the
activity of the Mayor and police, for Louisiana has in-
terceded with its judiciary to put criminal sanctions behind racial discrimination in public places. She may not
do so consistently with the Equal Protection Clause of
the Fourteenth Amendment.

The criminal penalty (60 days in jail and a $350 fine)
was imposed on these petitioners by Louisiana's judiciary. That action of the judiciary was state action. Such
are the holdings in *Shelley* v. *Kraemer,* 334 U.S. 1, and
*Barrows* v. *Jackson,* 346 U.S. 249. Those cases involved
restrictive covenants. *Shelley* v. *Kraemer* was a civil suit
to enjoin violation of a restrictive covenant by a Negro
purchaser. *Barrows* v. *Jackson* was a suit to collect damages for violating a restrictive covenant by selling residential property to a Negro. Those cases, like the present
one, were "property" cases. In those cases, as in the present one, the line was drawn at dealing with Negroes.
There, as here, no state legislature was involved, only the
state judiciary. The Court said in *Shelley* v. *Kraemer:*

"That the action of state courts and judicial officers in their official capacities is to be regarded as
action of the State within the meaning of the Fourteenth Amendment, is a proposition which has long
been established by decisions of this Court." 334
U.S., at 14.

The list of instances where action of the state judiciary
is state action within the meaning of the Fourteenth
Amendment is a long one. Many were noted in *Shelley*
v. *Kraemer,* 334 U.S., pp. 14-18. Most state convictions
in violation of the First, Fourth, or Fifth Amendment,
as incorporated in the Due Process Clause of the Fourteenth Amendment, have indeed implicated not the state
legislature but the state judiciary, or the state judiciary
and the state prosecutor and the state police. *Shelley* v.
*Kraemer*—and later *Barrows* v. *Jackson*—held that the
state judiciary, acting alone to enforce private discrimination against Negroes who desired to buy private property in residential areas, violated the Equal Protection
Clause of the Fourteenth Amendment.

Places of public accommodation such as retail stores,
restaurants, and the like render a "service which has
become a public interest" (*German Alliance Ins. Co.* v.
*Kansas, supra,* 408) in the manner of the innkeepers and
common carriers of old. The substance of the old common-law rules has no direct bearing on the decision
required in this case. Restaurateurs and owners of other
places of amusement and resort have never been subjected to the same duties as innkeepers and common carriers. But, what is important is that this whole body
of law was a response to the felt needs of the times that

spawned it. In our time the interdependence of people has greatly increased; the days of *laissez faire* have largely disappeared; men are more and more dependent on their neighbors for services as well as for housing and the other necessities of life. By enforcing this criminal mischief statute, invoked in the manner now before us, the Louisiana courts are denying some people access to the mainstream of our highly interdependent life solely because of their race. Yet, "If there is any one purpose of the Fourteenth Amendment that is wholly outside the realm of doubt, it is that the Amendment was designed to bar States from denying to some groups, on account of their race or color, any rights, privileges, and opportunities accorded to other groups." *Oyama* v. *California,* 332 U.S. 633, 649 (concurring opinion).

An innkeeper or common carrier has always been allowed to exclude drunks, criminals and diseased persons, but only because the public's interest in protecting his and his guests' health and property outweighs its interest in providing accommodations for this small group of travelers. As a general rule, innkeepers and carriers cannot refuse their services on account of race; though the rule developed in this country that they can provide "separate but equal" facilities. And for a period of our history even this court upheld state laws giving sanction to such a rule. Compare *Plessy* v. *Ferguson,* 163 U.S. 537, with *Gayle* v. *Browder,* 352 U.S. 903, affirming, 142 F. Supp. 707. But surely *Shelley* v. *Kraemer, supra,* and *Barrows* v. *Jackson, supra,* show that the day has passed when an innkeeper, carrier, housing developer, or retailer can draw a racial line, refuse service to some on account of color, and obtain the aid of a State in enforcing his personal bias by sending outlawed customers to prison or exacting fines from them.

Business, such as this restaurant, is still private property. Yet there is hardly any private enterprise that does not feel the pinch of some public regulation—from price control, to health and fire inspection, to zoning, to safety measures, to minimum wages and working conditions, to unemployment insurance. When the doors of a business are open to the public, they must be open to all regardless of race if *apartheid* is not to become engrained in our public places. It cannot by reason of the Equal Protection Clause become so engrained with the aid of state courts, state legislatures, or state police.

## II

There is even greater reason to bar a State through its judiciary from throwing its weight on the side of racial discrimination in the present case, because we deal here with a place of public accommodation under license from the State. This is the idea I expressed in *Garner* v. *Louisiana, supra,* where another owner of a restaurant refused service to a customer because he was a Negro. That view is not novel; it stems from the dissent of the first Mr. Justice Harlan in the *Civil Rights Cases,* 109 U.S. 3, 58-59:

> "In every material sense applicable to the practical enforcement of the Fourteenth Amendment, railroad corporations, keepers of inns, and managers of places of public amusement are agents or instrumentalities of the State, because they are charged with duties to the public, and are amenable, in respect of their duties and functions, to governmental

regulation. It seems to me that, within the principle settled in *Ex parte Virginia,* a denial, by these instrumentalities of the State, to the citizen, because of his race, of that equality of civil rights secured to him by law, is a denial by the State, within the meaning of the Fourteenth Amendment. If it be not, then that race is left, in respect of the civil rights in question, practically at the mercy of corporations and individuals wielding power under the States."

The nexus between the State and the private enterprise may be control, as in the case of a state agency. *Pennsylvania* v. *Board of Trusts,* 353 U.S. 230. Or the nexus may be one of numerous other devices. "State support of segregated schools through any arrangement, management, funds, or property cannot be squared" with the Equal Protection Clause. *Cooper* v. *Aaron,* 358 U.S. 1, 19. Cf. *Ghiotto* v. *Hampton,* 304 F.2d 320. A state-assisted enterprise serving the public does not escape its constitutional duty to serve all customers irrespective of race, even though its actual operation is in the hands of a lessee. *Burton* v. *Wilmington Parking Authority,* 365 U.S. 715. Cf. *Boynton* v. *Virginia,* 364 U.S. 454. State licensing and surveillance of a business serving the public also brings its service into the public domain. This restaurant needs a permit from Louisiana to operate; and during the existence of the license the State has broad powers of visitation and control. This restaurant is thus an instrumentality of the State since the State charges it with duties to the public and supervises its performance. The State's interest in and activity with regard to its restaurants extends far beyond any mere income-producing licensing requirement.

There is no constitutional way, as I see it, in which a State can license and superivse a business serving the public and endow it with the authority to manage that business on the basis of *apartheid* which is foreign to our Constitution.

# INDEX

233

# WILLIAM O. DOUGLAS

Born in Maine, Minnesota, in 1898, William O. Douglas grew up in Yakima, Washington. He received his law degree from Columbia Law School in 1925, was admitted to the New York Bar and practiced law in New York City. He was a faculty member of Columbia Law School from 1924 to 1928 and of the Yale Law School from 1928 to 1939, though on leave of absence in Washington, D.C., beginning in 1934. He was Chairman of the Securities and Exchange Commission when President Franklin Roosevelt nominated him to be an Associate Justice of the United States Supreme Court and took his seat on April 17, 1939. Since 1940 he has written twenty books, which include *Of Men and Mountains,* published in 1950, *A Living Bill of Rights,* 1961, and *Democracy's Manifesto,* 1962.